THE RIVER COLUMN

A NARRATIVE OF THE ADVANCE OF THE RIVER
COLUMN OF THE NILE EXPEDITIONARY
FORCE, AND ITS RETURN DOWN
THE RAPIDS

BY

MAJOR-GENERAL
HENRY BRACKENBURY, C.B.

LATE COMMANDING THE RIVER COLUMN;
FORMERLY PROFESSOR OF MILITARY HISTORY AT THE ROYAL
MILITARY ACADEMY, WOOLWICH; AUTHOR OF 'A
NARRATIVE OF THE ASHANTI WAR'

WITH MAPS
BY
MAJOR THE HON. F. L. L. COLBORNE

ROYAL IRISH RIFLES; LATE OF THE SURVEY
DEPARTMENT OF THE COLUMN

J. Perkins.
october 1885.

WILLIAM BLACKWOOD AND SONS
EDINBURGH AND LONDON
MDCCCLXXXV

PREFACE.

I HAVE written this simple narrative in the belief that the advance and return of four regiments of infantry through a hundred miles of cataracts and rapids in an enemy's country deserve, as a military operation, some permanent record, and because death has removed the only other officers possessing sufficient knowledge of all details to write that record with accuracy.

It would have been a pleasure to me to take this opportunity of praising those individuals to whom, in my opinion, such success as the Column attained is chiefly due;

but my position demands so strict a neutrality that I have thought it right to avoid all words of praise, lest in any case their accidental omission might appear to impute the semblance of blame.

HENRY BRACKENBURY.

London, *September* 1835.

CONTENTS.

LIST OF MAPS.

THE RIVER COLUMN.

———•———

CHAPTER I.

KORTI TO MERAWI—ADVANCED GUARD.

On the morning of the 24th December 24th Dec. 1884. 1884, I arrived at Korti, Lord Wolseley's headquarters—having up to that time been engaged as Deputy Adjutant and Quartermaster General under General Sir Redvers Buller, the chief of the staff, in the organisation of the Nile Expedition. The exact nature of Lord Wolseley's plans was not at that time known to me; but I knew that his original idea of moving the whole force by river to Berber and thence to Khartoum

A

had necessarily to be abandoned, and that, if Gordon were to be rescued within the period we had reason to hope he could hold out for, troops must be sent across the desert. That this was a more or less desperate venture, none of us could for a moment doubt; but it had to be made, if Gordon were to be saved; and in the four camel regiments, camel battery, camel - bearer company, camel field - hospital, and camel transport - companies, a force had been specially organised for this effort. It was not, however, till after General Buller's arrival at Korti, that the exact nature of Lord Wolseley's plan was made known to me, and the details of the scheme had then to be worked out.

The plan, in its bare outline, was as follows: The greater portion of the mounted troops, under Sir Herbert Stewart, was to advance across the desert from Korti to Metemmeh, establishing fortified posts at the wells along the route. Sir Charles Wilson was then, with a small escort of infantry, to proceed in Gordon's steamers to Khartoum, and, having communicated with Gordon, to return to Metemmeh. Upon his report the future conduct of the desert column would be framed. I do not know what instructions Sir Herbert Stewart may have received; but I do know that if Stewart had not been killed, and if Wilson had brought back word that Gordon was holding out, but in sore need, Stewart and the troops under him were capable of forcing their way to Gordon's assistance through any number of the enemy. And I know that if Wilson's report as to Gordon's power of holding out had been favourable, Lord Wolseley himself had intended to join Stewart, taking with him the remainder of the mounted troops and a force of infantry.

Simultaneously with the advance of the desert column under Stewart, a force was to be sent by river under command of General Earle to punish the murderers of Colonel Stewart and of the Consuls, and

to advance by Berber to co-operate with
Stewart's force in an attack on the Mahdi
before Khartoum, under Lord Wolseley's
personal command.

I was informed that Lord Wolseley had
selected me to be second in command of
this column and chief staff-officer to Major-
25th Dec. General Earle ; and on Christmas Day
General Buller set me free from my work
in his office—bringing in Colonel Wolseley, A.A.G., to replace me—and told me
to devote my whole time to organising
General Earle's column, as Lord Wolseley
wanted me to proceed at the earliest possible date with a battalion of infantry and
a few cavalry to establish an advanced
post at Hamdab, above the portion of
river marked in the map as the Gerendid cataract, and near the point (Dugiyet)
where the desert road from Berber strikes
the river. General Earle was at this time
at Dongola.

I had some few details to discuss with
Herbert Stewart. The cavalry of the ex-

pedition—five troops—was to be evenly
divided between us; and the Royal Engineers, who had reached Korti in boats, were,
with their equipment, to be divided into two
portions—one to accompany the desert and
one the river column. We had no difficulty
in settling matters amicably.

The first battalion of the South Staffordshire Regiment—the battalion which had first
ascended the river in whalers—was to lead
the advance up the river. I had accompanied them on their start from Gemai
dockyard, above the second cataract, to
Sarras; and had congratulated Colonel Eyre
upon the strange chance which had given
him, as the boat at the head of his column,
that bearing the number 38, the old number
of his regiment; and knowing what a keen
soldier he was, I was glad to have him with
me now.[1]

In making the preparations for a start, it

[1] Another curious coincidence was the fact that the first boat
taken up through the great gate of the second cataract, under
the superintendence of Colonel Butler, bore the number 69—the
number of his old regiment, of whose " Records" he is the historian.

was found that the original liberal allowance of boat-gear with which the troops had started had been sadly reduced by the journey up the river, and that we could not count upon more than eight oars and two poles per boat. And as the supplies of food brought up by the Staffords were being taken in great quantities for the desert column, we had to content ourselves with thirty days' boat rations for the present. In a memo. written to Colonel Eyre on the 26th, authorising an issue of soap, I said : " In this and every similar issue, you must impress upon your men the necessity of economy. They have many weeks, probably some months, of work yet before them, and all supplies are limited in quantity."

At this time Colonel Colvile was at Merawi, or rather at Abu Dom, which is to Merawi what Southwark is to London. With him was the Vakeel of the Mudirieh of Dongola, Gaudet Bey, with some 400 of the Mudir's troops. The Mudir was supposed to be collecting supplies for us; and

I entered into telegraphic correspondence with Colonel Colvile, telling him the quantities of barley, dourra, dourra - stalk, and firewood we required to be ready for us on our arrival.

On Sunday, the 28th December, at 2 P.M., 28th Dec. the Staffords, 545 of all ranks, entered their fifty boats. I had issued orders previously to the following effect: " From the time of leaving Korti, the company will be the unit by which boats will work. The utmost efforts must be made to keep companies together. In every case an officer will be with the last boat of the company, and it will be his duty to urge on, and assist where necessary, any boats of his company which may be falling behind." Working on this principle, the Staffords started, and in thirty-one minutes their last boat was under way. It was the first time that a whole battalion had moved together, and as it was the first forward movement beyond Korti, it was full of interest. Two boats, containing a detachment, 26th Company,

R.E., under Captain Blackburn, left at the same time.

29th Dec. Early on the 29th half a troop of 19th Hussars, under Captain Aylmer, twenty-six of all ranks, and thirty horses, marched to overtake the Staffords, taking with them the horses and camels of my own party; and in the afternoon I started in the Monarch steam-launch with Major Slade, D.A.A.G., Intelligence Department; Captain Beaumont, K.R.R., officer for signalling; and D.A.C.G. Boyd, of the Commissariat.

Before starting I said good-bye to two old friends whom I was never destined to see again, Herbert Stewart and St Leger Herbert. We had all served together in South Africa, and at the storming of Sekukuni's fighting koppie. We had lived together and travelled together for many a weary league. Stewart had succeeded me as military secretary to Lord Wolseley when I went to join the Viceroy's staff in India. St Leger Herbert had been my companion on the staff in Cyprus as well. I do not know which was the keener soldier of the two. If ever a man loved fighting, it was St Leger Herbert; and Stewart's and my last words together were the mutually expressed hope that each of us would meet the enemy in force, and make an end of it in one good fight.

At 5 P.M. we overtook the Staffords and Hussars about twenty miles from Korti, and bivouacked for the night on the left bank at the village of Kureir, opposite Hanneck.

The following morning, 30th, we advanced 30th Dec. to Abu Dom. Having selected a site for our bivouac, about half a mile above a strong fort that had been built by native labourers on the designs of the Vakeel, and below which the native troops were hutted, I visited Colonel Colvile, who was living in a grass hut on the river-bank close to the landing-place, surrounded by groaning camels and by natives anxious to bargain, or clamouring for payment for supplies or camels purchased for the desert column.

I now held an interview in Colonel Colvile's hut with the Vakeel, who was living on board a dahabeeyah close by, at which interview the Turkish major commanding the troops assisted. I told them our wants in the matter of supplies. Many difficulties were made, but ultimately all we wanted was promised, both in cattle, dourra, dourra-stalk, wood, and wheat, The exceptions were barley and flour—the Vakeel assuring me that the first was not in existence, and the latter not to be obtained in any large quantities, owing to the scarcity of grindstones. This we found to be true : there were only two large grindstones, of the kind which are turned one upon the other, in all the district; the flour for the use of each family being made by the women of the family, by pounding or rubbing with a stone a small handful at a time of wheat or dourra placed in a hollowed-out stone. The result of the interview, in spite of all promises, left on my mind the conviction that Gaudet Bey and the Major meant to be obstructive, and had no intention of doing for us any more than they could help; and I gave the Vakeel to understand that we must have what we wanted, and that the military commander must now reign supreme.

Colvile, Slade, and I then proceeded up the river in the picket-boat, with a view to selecting a camping-ground at Belal; but, finding we should not have time to get so far, we returned to Abu Dom. Immediately on our return we were informed that a messenger from Gordon had arrived, and that the Vakeel had telegraphed the fact to the Mudir. As this was in direct opposition to the instructions given by me in the morning, that no telegrams were to be sent unless first submitted to Colonel Colvile, I sent for the Vakeel; and on my saying I must report him to Lord Wolseley, he replied that he did not care—he was not Lord Wolseley's Vakeel. As I found that he had not collected the supplies which he had promised to collect on the opposite bank for our troops, and had replied, when asked about it, that he had not time to discuss the matter, I telegraphed to General Buller that I thought we should do better to send the Vakeel away, and appoint the Kasheef of Belal, Mohammed Effendi Wad Kenaish, to act in his place. The same night I received a telegram from General Buller saying that a very civil message had been sent to the Vakeel requesting him to come to Korti, and one from Sir C. Wilson, asking me to tell the Vakeel that Lord Wolseley wished to consult him on matters of importance, and begged he would go there by the picket-boat next day.

I then saw the messenger from Gordon. He was a man who had been sent by Colvile with a letter from Lord Wolseley; and he brought back that now historical letter of three words, "Khartoum all right, 14th December, C. G. Gordon." He told me that when he left Khartoum all was well there, and that provisions were sufficient, though not plentiful. On his way back he had remained six days in the Mahdi's camp.

Sickness was prevalent among the enemy, but there was no lack of food. He told me that Hashm el Moos was at Wady Bishara on the 21st December with three steamers, having loaded two steamers with provisions and sent them to Khartoum. He then added in great secrecy that Gordon had confided to him a message that we were to come quickly,—not to divide our force or leave Berber behind, but to take Berber and come by the right bank.

That night of bivouac was rendered hideous by the Mudir's troops. They had a semicircle of sentries from the fort to the river enclosing their huts and Colvile's camels; and they shouted the equivalent of "all's well" without cessation. Each sentry had a number, and as soon as No. 1 had called out "No. 1, all's well," No. 2 shouted "No. 2, all's well," and so on till the last number was reached, when No. 1 began again. This continued through the whole night. Colvile was used to it, and did not mind.

On the morning of the 31st the Vakeel and Gordon's messenger went off together to Korti in the Monarch picket-boat, Lieutenant Tyler, R.N., who was in charge, having great difficulty in carrying out his orders to keep them apart. I informed General Buller that I had appointed Mohammed Wad Kenaish to act in the Vakeel's place, instead of the major whom the Vakeel had named; and was instructed in reply that I should have accepted the deputy appointed by the Vakeel, and that my action amounted to taking the government of the country into our hands, which was not desirable. It was proposed to admonish the Vakeel seriously, and send him back. I urged by telegraph his not being sent back; but was informed that it would not do to start in one portion of the Mudirieh a policy different from that prevailing elsewhere. I vainly represented that part of this portion of the Mudirieh was in rebellion, and taxes could not be collected; that the Vakeel confessed himself unable to

punish the persons who cut the telegraph;
that, according to the Vakeel, El Zain, with
some of the Mahdi's dervishes, was at
Hamdab, and that these were reasons why
the military authority should be paramount
here. I only found that I was uselessly
kicking against the pricks. Lord Wolseley
did not consider any of my reasons sufficient,
and I was told the Vakeel would be sent
back with General Earle.[1]

Meanwhile, throughout the day the Staffords with their boats had been employed
in bringing over to the left bank the supplies collected in the Shoona or Government store on the right bank. Had
I passed on, leaving the supplies in the
Shoona, the bringing them over to the left
bank might have been indefinitely postponed; and in the present temper of the
Mudir's authorities, I did not feel sure
the supplies would ever reach us. I considered it important to show that we meant

[1] The Vakeel afterwards told Colonel Colvile and myself that
he was at this time acting under orders from the Mudir of
Dongola to give us as little help as possible.

to have what we wanted, and were capable of helping ourselves, if need be; and this action had an undoubtedly good effect.

In the course of the day I presented Said Hassan, the Sheikh of Amri Island and King of Zowarah, with a robe of honour in Lord Wolseley's name. This monarch had joined the Shagiyeh in rebellion against the Egyptians in the previous summer, and had been badly wounded in the arm when fighting against the Mudir's troops at Korti. He had since thought better of it; and when, shortly before, Suleiman Wad Gamr had sent to his island to bring him to Birti, he had, according to his own story, escaped and fled to us. This noble conduct I had been instructed to reward in what was certainly a conspicuous manner; for when the old gentleman was clothed in a scarlet cloth robe, a crimson fez, a sword very much gilt with sundry gorgeous tassels, and a pair of red slippers, he was as like a monkey on a barrel-organ as anything I ever saw. But he was a king, and the act I had been performing was one with which every reader of the Scriptures is familiar. King Said's first act was to beg for money for himself and his ragged retinue, and to try to drive as hard a bargain with me as he could. I promised him finally a pound a-day for himself and his followers, provided he would help us with labour and supplies when we reached his country—payment to be contingent on results. He never was of the slightest use to us; and as, when we returned to Abu Dom, he did not hesitate to return among the rebels, I have little doubt that he had only followed the traditionary policy of the Soudanese sheikhs, to have some of a family on each side in a war, so that, whichever side wins, there may be some in power to intercede for those on the beaten side. In fact, so well is this policy recognised among them, that the members of the family who have been on the wrong side are thought none the worse of for their apparent treason.

B

About seven o'clock in the evening, telegraphic communication with Korti was interrupted. I did not learn this till nearly nine, and then at once sent out an officer of Engineers with a few Hussars and a native linesman to repair the line. They returned about 2.30 A.M., having found it cut about eight miles from our camp, and traces of camels leading into the desert. They had repaired the line.

1st Jan.
1885.

On New Year's Day the Staffords continued and completed the work of bringing over the supplies from the Shoona; and I rode with Major Slade and Captain Beaumont about eight miles, to Belal, at the foot of the Gerendid cataract, and selected a bivouac. On the way we passed close to a remarkable cluster of pyramids, many of which have crumbled away into gravel mounds, a few retaining their pyramidal form. Their bases are buried, but not deep, in the sand, and the highest stands about sixty feet above the present level. They stand in irregular rows. They are made of blocks of pudding-stone, of which there is a large quantity in the neighbour-hood, faced with one layer of blocks of sandstone. No native has the vaguest idea of their age. They are undoubtedly tombs; their neighbourhood has been used as a graveyard from time immemorial, and is so now. I inquired at Belal if any curios-ities, scarabæi, clay figures, or antiquities of any sort were ever found there, offering to purchase them at a good price; but was assured nothing had ever been found. On the opposite bank of the river, about equally distant from its present bed, stands another cluster of similar pyramids near the hill known as Jebel Barkal, in which a temple is hewn.

On New Year's night we dined outside Colonel Colvile's hut. In addition to the *menu* furnished by our rations, we had eggs and chickens, pumpkin, and a plum-pudding, a most delicious melon, a bottle of cham-pagne, and a tot of whisky. The English mail arrived bringing us letters and Christmas cards, and we sat up till late, speculating on what the year would bring forth. Then saying good-bye to Colvile, we of the river column sought our beds on the soft, clean, yellow sand by the side of the sleeping troops.

CHAPTER II.

MERAWI TO HAMDAB—ADVANCED POST.

ON the morning of the 2d, at six o'clock, 2d Jan. the Staffords moved off in their boats, the Hussars covering the advance along the bank. They arrived at Belal in the afternoon. Slade, with an escort, rode over to Hamdab to select a camping-ground for our concentration; the rest of our party remained at Belal. The Kasheef, Mohammed Wad Kenaish, brought us excellent wheaten cakes, honey, and melons, with milk both sweet and sour, in which latter condition only the natives seem to drink it. The people brought dates and milk and bread for sale to the troops.

Slade received information that there

were about 600 rebels at Birti, under
Moussa, the son of Abu Hegel, sheikh of
the Robatab tribe.   Moussa, it was reported,
had been made an Emir by the Mahdi, and
was anxious to advance towards Hamdab.
Suleiman Wad Gamr, sheikh of the Monassir tribe, was said to have objected to this
advance, and to have left Birti on the 29th
December with the intention of proceeding to
Berber, and reporting the matter to Mohammed el Kheir, the Mahdi's Emir of Berber.

We also learnt the particulars of a raid
which had been made much nearer to us on
the last day of the year, and of which we
had received information at Abu Dom.   El
Zain, a well known robber chief, with forty
followers, had raided from the wells of El
Koua, thirty miles out on the road from
Dugiyet to Berber, and had captured nearly
200 camels which were grazing in the desert
about two hours' march from the river.   A
large number of these camels belonged to
the Kasheef of Belal.

We were now, it appeared, really begin-

ning to approach a hostile country. Thirty
miles in front of us was a force of Monassir and Robatab ready to fight, under a
commander who wanted to lead them on;
and thirty miles on our right flank was a
famous raider with a number of followers
more bold than numerous. We had been
so long sitting still without a prospect of a
fight, that we had begun almost to disbelieve
in the possibility of one; but our prospects
were apparently brightening.

We had a pleasant enough spot for our
bivouac, with good anchorage, and a grove
of palm-trees close by. But we noticed
that the desert had now become rocky, and
the rocks came close down to the river.
The fine open sandy plain, so favourable
for the development of modern infantry
fire, so fatal to the Arab rush, had disappeared. We had entered into the region of
rocks and cataracts, that we were to carry
with us almost to the furthest limits of
the country of the Monassir.

On the 3d we again advanced, our lead- 3d Jan.

ing boats reaching their camping-ground at Hamdab at one o'clock, and the last boat closing up to them by two; and this in spite of Omar, the sheikh of Duaim, whom we had chartered as a pilot, running Colonel Eyre's boat on a rock. We found no cataract, only a very rapid stream between rocks, against which the men were able to row. And so the Gerendid cataract,[1] of which we had a picture in the Intelligence Department publications, did not exist; and we began to congratulate ourselves on the prospect of an easy ascent to Berber.

News reached us that a party of fifty dervishes (the generic name for the Mahdi's followers, dressed in his patchwork uniform) was on the right bank opposite Ooli Island; and that El Zain at El Koua had been reinforced by forty men from Berber. We were now beyond Dugiyet, and the point, marked by a solitary dom-palm, where the chief desert-track from Berber strikes the

---

[1] No native of the district had ever heard this name. The local name is the rapids of Hajar Oolad Gurbar.

Nile. Under these circumstances the wells of El Koua and Bir Sani became an important point for our consideration, as the raid made towards the river might at any time be repeated, and our convoys from Abu Dom, of which the first arrived to-day, might be molested. But my handful of cavalry was too small to attempt any counterstroke in that direction, and I telegraphed to Korti asking for more cavalry, and expressing the desire that the Mudir's troops, whom I had been directed not to move, should cross the river, and encamp on the opposite bank to us, so as to prevent small parties of dervishes, such as we were informed were near Ooli Island, firing across the river into our camp at night.

Not liking the camp selected by Slade, 4th Jan. I rode out on the morning of the 4th and chose another site about a mile farther up stream, with good anchorage, and an excellent position for a small defensive work, on the site of an old mud fort placed on a rocky spur jutting out into the Nile, and commanding the river and the camp. We then rode on to Jebel Kulgeili, about five miles to the front, and ascended the mountain. From it we could see for many miles in every direction; but only about three miles of actual river were visible beyond the mountain, as the islands over- lap and close the view near Ooli Island. We could see enough, however, to assure us that there was nothing to stop the boats' progress from Hamdab to Ooli.

As far as Belal we had been travelling through a rich country with much cultiva- tion; at Belal, as already stated, the rocks came down to near the river, and from Belal to Hamdab but little cultivation ex- isted. Beyond Hamdab the amount of cultivation still further diminished, and the people, who up to Hamdab had been friend- ly, became more shy, several houses being deserted. But from Kulgeili to Ooli there was not a sign of life. One or two strips of neglected cultivation existed, but every hovel was deserted. Hamdab marked

the limits of territory within which the
Mudir had collected taxes since the rebellion began; and those beyond that limit,
not having paid taxes, had doubtless guilty
consciences, and the fear bred thereof. We
read, however, to those of them whom we
could assemble between Belal and Kulgeili,
Lord Wolseley's proclamation of friendli-
ness to the Shagiyeh, and left copies of it
with them.

In the afternoon General Earle arrived
with his aide-de-camp, Lieut. St Aubyn, and
Brigade-Major, Major Boyle, and assumed
command. He brought with him Lord Wolseley's instructions, which had been shown
to me before leaving Korti. In them he was
informed that his force was to consist of—

    One squadron 19th Hussars;
    The Staffordshire Regiment;
    The Royal Highlanders;
    The Duke of Cornwall's Light Infantry;
    The Gordon Highlanders;
    A battery of Egyptian Artillery;
    The Egyptian Camel Corps;

Headquarters and 300 camels of the
11th Transport Company;
and that in addition another regiment would
be placed at his disposal to form posts between
Merawi and Abu Hamed.   He was to concentrate at Abu Hamed, and advance thence
as soon as he had collected a hundred days'
supplies per man.   Major Rundle, who had
a large quantity of rations at Korosko, had
undertaken to have a convoy of supplies at
Abu Hamed four days after General Earle's
arrival there.   After filling up with supplies
at Abu Hamed, General Earle was to advance upon Berber; and having secured
that place, to endeavour to forward as
many supplies as possible to the force
which would have proceeded by land to
Khartoum.   A portion of the Mudir's
troops was told off to accompany General
Earle's force.   He might use them as he
thought fit, but it was suggested he should
employ them to collect supplies in the
Monassir country.   He was to treat all
tribes as friends (except the Monassir) if

they would meet his advances; if not, he was to enforce his demands. The Monassir were only to be treated as friends if they would give up the murderers of Colonel Stewart and his party. He was to occupy Abu Hamed and Berber, and such other places as might be necessary for the safety of his line; and to consider it of first importance to place 75,000 rations at Shendy at the disposal of the force operating by the desert as quickly as possible.

To the above military instructions some political instructions were added for General Earle in his dealings with the various tribes. The sheikhs, he was told, might be informed that the English policy was, in the first place, to restore peace and tranquillity to the country, and then to establish some form of native government which would be acceptable to the people. The English Government did not intend to interfere with the property or just rights of any one. All persons wishing to submit, with the exception of the murderers of Colonel

Stewart and his party, and their accomplices, would be well received and pardoned if they gave in their submission at once; but those persisting in rebellion would receive the punishment they deserved.

For the better carrying out of these instructions, letters in Arabic, addressed to the sheikhs of the various tribes, had been prepared; and General Earle was instructed, before entering each district, to send one of these letters to the sheikh or tribe to whom it was addressed. A special proclamation, offering a reward for the apprehension of Suleiman Wad Gamr and Fakri Wad Etman, the instigator and perpetrator of Stewart's murder, was to be circulated only when it should be known that Suleiman Wad Gamr had fled.

In the course of the afternoon a telegram arrived, instructing the General that he was not to advance beyond Hamdab until he could do so with his whole force. Lord Wolseley also wished him to avoid reconnaissances as much as possible,—deprecat-

ing reconnaissances from a stationary force,
as the reconnoitrers must in the end retire to their force, and such a retirement is
often magnified by natives into a defeat;
and as it was of importance to prevent any
opening being given for such a rumour.

On the 5th January Major Flood marched 5th Jan.
into camp with a troop and a half of Hussars,
completing the squadron to 91 sabres; and
the troops were employed preparing the
newly selected camp. We were now nineteen miles from the telegraph station at
Abu Dom; but there was lying along the
ground between us, and in the river at
Merawi, much wire belonging to the old
Berber line, which had crossed the desert
from Dugiyet, and Lieutenant Stuart, R.E.,
was already at work getting poles cut and
erected by native labour. Meanwhile we
had established a daily camel-post with
Abu Dom; and to-day we received by it
the welcome news from General Buller
that Herbert Stewart had successfully established posts at Gakdul and Howeiyet, had

found plenty of water, grass, and firewood, and would return with the convoy to-day. His expedition to Gakdul, we were told, had been a complete surprise. No opposition had been offered, and he had captured several prisoners.

6th Jan.   On the 6th, in a most unpleasant dust-storm, the troops moved into their new camp. A market was at once established; and the natives brought in a fair supply of milk, dates, dourra-bread, and other products of the country. So well satisfied with our treatment of them were the natives, that several of them afterwards followed us up the country, bringing dates to sell. Three of these met with their death at the hands of some Monassir, near Kirbekan, a few days after the action there.

The daily record from this date to the 23d January would have but little general interest. The troops for the column continued to arrive at Abu Dom and Hamdab; and we were busily occupied in perfecting our arrangements for the advance.

The organisation of our force necessitated my making one trip to Korti, and several to Abu Dom; and General Earle had to go once to Abu Dom to bring the Vakeel to book. Of that organisation I propose to speak in the next chapter.

Only one or two matters of external interest occurred during this period. The sheikh of Ooli, or rather a younger brother of the sheikh, stating that the sheikh was lame and unable to walk, came into our camp and asked for the protection promised under Lord Wolseley's proclamation to the Shagiyeh. This he was promised on condition that he helped us to obtain supplies.

At 1.45 A.M. on the 13th, a report arrived 13th Jan. from Colvile, saying that Omar, the sheikh of Duaim, whom we had employed as a pilot for a short time, but subsequently dismissed as incompetent, had met two men at Belal, who stated that they had accompanied a force of 1000 men from Berber to the wells of Bak, half-way between Bir Sani and El Koua; that the force was armed with

rifles, and had a great quantity of ammunition, and that it was intended to attack
our camp in the early morning. Cavalry
patrols were at once sent out in the direction of the Berber road, and other military
precautions taken. Nothing came of it;
and when traced to its source, the rumour
appeared to be a concoction of Omar's own,
based upon the fact that two men had
arrived at Belal from Bir Sani, bringing the
news of a reinforcement of 50 men to El
Zain, and a report of a force of 1000 men
having marched from Berber, under Abdul
Majid Wad el Lekalik, to reinforce the
enemy at Birti.

It was, however, evident that unless
something were done to stop El Zain,
rumours of this sort would occur from time
to time; and General Earle decided to ask
Lord Wolseley's permission to make a raid
upon this cluster of wells. The permission being accorded, it was decided to make
the raid shortly before our advance up the
river, allowing only sufficient time for the

horses to have a couple of days' rest afterwards. Accordingly, on the 17th January
the Egyptian Camel Regiment, with twenty
camels of the Egyptian battery, carrying
all the available camel water-tins, were
brought from Abu Dom to Hamdab, it
being given out that the water-tanks were
being brought up to be overhauled by the
Engineers; and orders were issued that on
Sunday the 18th the General would inspect
the Engineers, the Hussars, and the Camel
Corps in fighting order, with two days'
rations, water, &c., as if ready to march
into action. Major Flood, 19th Hussars,
who was to command the party, and Major
Slade, of the Intelligence Department, were
taken into the secret. No one else but
General Earle and myself had an inkling
of what was intended.

Our information was to the effect that
the wells of El Koua, where great numbers
of cattle and camels of the Monassir were
said to be, were seven hours distant (this
time would not represent more than twenty-

eight miles); that the wells of Bir Sani were some two hours farther on, with the wells of Bak intervening; and that El Zain, with a party of dervishes, variously estimated at from 100 to 150, lived, with their flocks and herds, and the camels they had captured, on a hill called Jebel Katete, about two miles from Bir Sani, coming down to the wells for water.

Major Flood's instructions were to proceed with the Hussars (about 60 sabres) and Camel Corps (about 90 rifles) to the wells of El Koua, and, if possible, to Bak and Bir Sani, to surprise the Arabs, take them prisoners, burn their dwellings, and capture their camels and cattle. He was instructed to strike a blow at El Zain if possible, but not to be drawn into a serious engagement; and it was left to his judgment whether he would proceed beyond El Koua. Major Slade procured a guide, and was placed at Major Flood's disposal.

18th Jan. The parade was held on Sunday at 1 P.M. The Engineers, having been inspected, were dismissed. The mounted troops were told the General would inspect them after a short march; and they moved off into the desert, striking into a *khor* which led them by a short cut into the Berber-Dugiyet road, some five miles from Dugiyet. The secret had been well kept in camp. But it must have got out—probably through the guide, who has since joined the Mahdi—for there on the road were the unmistakable traces of the recent passage of a camel from Dugiyet in the direction of the wells. Flood marched till near midnight, and then halted about eight miles short of El Koua. He started again at 4 A.M., and reached a cultivated *khor* (El Koua), where he found traces of hasty flight, but no cattle or camels. The wells gave barely sufficient water for thirty horses; the water he had with him was little more than enough for the men. The distance he had already travelled he estimated at thirty-five miles. He pushed on three miles to the end of the cultivated *khor*, where the rocks closed

19th Jan.

in and the ground became bad for cavalry;
and then, considering the distance and the
scarcity of water, he considered it advisable
not to go farther; burned some of the
Monassir huts, carried off some grain, and
returned the same night to Hamdab.

The raid had not had the result hoped
for; but it was sufficient to keep El Zain
quiet as long as we were anywhere within
striking distance of El Koua.

CHAPTER III.

HAMDAB—ORGANISATION.

THE chief care of a General in the organ- _{5th to 23d} Jan. isation of a force for active service is to ensure to his troops a sufficient supply of food and ammunition. This requires a sufficiency of transport, which again requires food for the transport animals. It may be assumed, as a general rule, that troops start properly clothed and armed, so that a supply of clothing and arms is only required when an expedition is likely to be prolonged.

When a General has secured for his troops the reasonable certainty of the necessary food and ammunition, he is at liberty to turn his mind to other questions of organisation, fore-

most in importance among which is the care
of his sick and wounded, and, in all ordinary
expeditions, the evacuation of the sick and
wounded from his field-hospitals to hospitals
upon the line of communication. It may
safely be said that these questions require
far more time and elaboration of detail than
the strategical and tactical questions; and
the system now prevailing in all European
armies is to give to a General in command
of an expedition a Chief of the Staff, who re-
lieves him of this detail, and of all the minor
details of camp routine, leaving the General
in command free to weigh the value of the
reports made by his intelligence department,
and to decide by what means, strategical
and tactical, he can obtain the greatest advantage over his enemy. This system
ensures to the General in command time for
thought, relief from small worrying cares,
and leisure to mature his plans of campaign
and of battle.

In the present case, the river column
had some peculiar advantages in its favour,

and some peculiar disadvantages to contend
with. In the first and great matter of food
for the troops, we were certain of its not
failing for nearly three months. All our
infantry leaving Korti brought one hundred
days' food per man in their boats,—food,
supposed to be of the best quality, specially
prepared and packed in England. All
other troops coming up in boats brought
as many days' supply as they could carry,
in addition to loads of material for their
special services. Every effort was made
to economise these supplies by obtaining
cattle and native flour. Troops leaving
Korti brought with them "way rations"
sufficient to last to Abu Dom. There
native bakers supplied them with bread
baked from native flour, and fresh meat
was killed for them. On arrival at Hamdab, they found a commissariat bakery,
which we established immediately on arrival, by building four ovens in the river
bank, each able to turn out nearly six hundred loaves a-day ; and a cattle depot, which

was kept supplied by local purchase. We were thus enabled to start from Hamdab with our supplies of biscuit and preserved meat almost untouched.

As originally intended in the orders given to General Earle, when he left Korti at the beginning of the year, we were to have a battalion of infantry for the special purpose of forming posts between Abu Dom and Abu Hamed, which would have greatly facilitated the forwarding of convoys of cattle after the column from Abu Dom; 15th Jan. but on the 15th, fresh orders were received to the effect that it would not be possible to give to General Earle a fifth battalion to occupy posts, that the General of communication would not establish any line of communication beyond Abu Dom, and that the river force was to be a flying column. We should therefore have to depend for food upon the supplies we could take with us from Abu Dom, upon whatever we could buy or capture in the country we were about to enter, and upon the promised convoy

from Korosko, which was to meet us at
Abu Hamed.

But we had not only to consider how to
supply the European troops with food. We
had to supply some 200 Egyptian troops,
and 150 natives, mostly Aden camel-drivers,
and to feed about 150 horses and 530 camels.
The Egyptian soldiers, Camel Corps, and
Artillery, agreed without a murmur to their
ration being confined to 1 lb. meat and 1 lb.
flour, if they were allowed a small sum, which
was settled at half a piastre (about 1¼d.)
daily, to supplement their ration by the purchase of vegetables or any native delicacy.
The Aden camel-drivers also consented to
forego their authorised ration of sugar, salt,
and tea or coffee; so that we were enabled
to reserve all our groceries for the European troops and Egyptian officers.

The horses—Egyptian cavalry horses—
which had been handed over to the 19th
Hussars at Wady Halfa, and the ponies of the
staff and regimental officers, were in hard
serviceable condition; but to keep them in

condition, they must not be reduced below their ration of 10 lb. of grain daily, to be supplemented by such green forage as could be procured. And this meant 1500 lb. of grain daily, or five camel-loads; for we found that 300 lb. is as heavy a load as camels in good condition will, on the average, carry for several days in succession.

The Camel Corps and the Artillery had sufficient regimental transport to carry six days' rations for themselves, and six days' forage, at a daily ration of 8 lb. of grain for each camel; but all the grain for horses, all further reserve of grain for the Egyptian camels, and all the grain for the Eleventh Transport Company, had to be carried by the 350 camels of that company, which had also to carry their own European staff, with their kits, the kits of the Aden drivers, the equipment of the Hussars, certain headquarter baggage and office material, a large number of iron water-tanks—brought up in case we should be compelled to make a flanking movement to turn a position by the desert, —and all the flour for the native troops. We were fairly well off for transport; but we were going into an enemy's country, where no supplies were likely to be forthcoming by purchase. It was said to be a very barren country also, and we must anticipate that the small store of grain kept by the natives would be either carried off or concealed, so that it was a matter of vital importance to take the utmost possible quantity of flour and grain with us.

As it was, we were enabled to start from Hamdab, taking 24th February as the day from which the start was made, with the following supplies : about eighty-five days' boat rations for the whole European force, with the exception of sugar and salt, of which we were on very short rations throughout. The ration of sugar was reduced even before we left Hamdab from two and a half to one and a half ounces; and the ration of salt was reduced to a quarter of an ounce, and only issued on days when fresh meat was served out. This quantity of eighty-five days' supply was what was represented by the number of

cases of the various kinds of food ; but, before leaving Hamdab, we had become aware
that in certain items, especially biscuit, preserved vegetables, rice, oatmeal, and tobacco, considerable deductions must be
made for goods damaged by water, owing
to defective packing, or rather defective
closing of the tin cases, and to the exposure
to wet to which large quantities of cases had
been subject in leaky or damaged boats on
the way from Sarras to Korti. We estimated
the probable loss in biscuit alone at thirty
per cent, almost all the " cabin biscuit"
being bad ; and accordingly we arranged
that the convoy from Korosko was to bring
to Abu Hamed supplies in the following
proportions : meat, tea, lime-juice, pepper,
one ration each ; preserved vegetables, one
and a half ; biscuit, sugar, and salt, two
rations each. The great loss in sugar and
salt was due chiefly to their having been
packed in bags, not waterproof, which had
become wet; and partly, especially in sugar,
to thefts by natives at the various portages

along our long line of communication from Alexandria to Korti.

For the natives we started with sixty days' supply of flour, and forty days' supply of unground wheat, which could either be converted into flour, or be used for the horses, if the supply of grain should fail. We hoped to collect cattle and sheep, or to get these sent up after us, in sufficient numbers to supply the natives daily with fresh meat; and as a matter of fact, that supply did not fail us till we had reached Hebbeh, a month after our start: up to that date we were successful in supplying all the troops with fresh meat, and our preserved meat was almost untouched.

For the horses we started with nearly forty days' grain. More could not be carried for want of transport. The camels, it was evident from the first, must go short of grain, and subsist on the growing forage, unless we could obtain grain in large quantities from the country we were about to enter.

For firewood we must trust to the local
supply for the day's wants : our transport
would not admit of our carrying on from
each bivouac more than sufficient for the
following day's needs, both boats and camels
being loaded up with full loads.

Such was our provision for the feeding of
the troops and animals. As regards ammunition, each gun had a hundred rounds,
and about 280 rounds for every rifle was
carried in the boats.

Our transport was in good condition.
The boats, in spite of their rough work on
the way up, were serviceable. They had
mostly been overhauled at Korti. Many of
them bore honourable scars in the shape
of tin patches, and there was rather a lack
of paint, but they were fit for work. Our
camels were in sound, serviceable order,
and their saddles were in good condition.

The next work which demanded attention was the organisation for the care of the
sick and wounded. The material for a field-
hospital of 200 beds had already been for-

warded to Abu Dom; but it was manifest to me, upon a cursory inspection, that it was upon a scale unsuited for our river expedition. Twenty hospital marquees were luxuries that we could not afford to carry; meat-covers and meat-skewers, however valuable elsewhere, were out of place here; large pewter measures and beer-taps still more so, in a land where no beer is. Pairs of bellows might possibly be useful, though it was doubtful; but coffee-mills could not help us, where there was no coffee. Sheets and pillows might be of great comfort, but they could only be taken in such small quantities as to be available for the worst cases; and so on through a long list, including blue waistcoats and trousers. In fact, all superfluous gear, to use the sailors' favourite word, must be abandoned—sacrificed to the stern necessity of utilising every particle of available transport for the carriage of food and ammunition.

Accordingly, I visited Korti, and there saw Surgeon-General O'Nial, the principal

D

medical officer of the expedition, and Surgeon-Major Harvey, who was selected as
senior medical officer of the river column.
They met me in the fairest way. I agreed,
on General Earle's part, to give them one
boat for each of the eight sections of the
field - hospital, and a ninth boat for the
senior medical officer, in which he could
take extra comforts for the sick, and to
furnish a sufficient number of men to make
up, with the men of the Medical Staff
Corps, crews for the boats. I undertook
that, if tentage was necessary, it should be
provided from the tents carried by the
troops in their boats. They agreed to
reduce the equipment, so that each section
for twenty-five patients should be carried
in one boat—a few luxuries such as con-
densed milk, champagne, lime - juice, &c.,
being carried by the senior medical officer.
Surgeon-Major Harvey proceeded to Abu
Dom, and superintended the revision of the
equipment, and its stowage in the whalers;
the crews for the whalers were sent down

from Hamdab. And throughout the campaign, two sections of this field-hospital accompanied each infantry battalion.

The resources of the field-hospital were made available to the utmost by the abandonment of all rules of red tape. Medical officers of corps were granted the power of admission to and discharge from the hospital, and were authorised to draw from the field-hospital at all times whatever was wanted to keep their regimental medical equipment complete.

We had no means, nor was there time at our disposal, for forming a bearer company to carry wounded out of action; but it was arranged that the eight stretchers of each battalion should accompany the battalion into action, carried by the bandsmen of the battalion. Each corps was to carry its own sick in its own boats, and the sick of mounted corps were to be carried in the boats of the battalion to which they were attached for rations. For it is one of the penalties of a flying column that it must carry forward with it, and cannot leave behind or send back, its sick and wounded.

A paymaster was sent to us with about £10,000 in money. We spent about £1500 in buying supplies, in native labour, &c., before leaving Hamdab; but from that time forward Major Mackie, our paymaster, had an easy time, for money was useless in an arid desert where there were no sellers and nothing to buy.

A veterinary surgeon accompanied the transport.

Only a few days before we left Hamdab, the telegraph was extended to an office in our fort there. This was a great boon, as it saved much time and labour hitherto expended in sending our messages to and receiving them from Abu Dom, nineteen miles away. The country was quite impracticable for heliographic signalling, owing to the absence of marked high hills, and the presence of a succession of low ridges.

Before the 24th of January a number of

Canadian voyageurs joined the column, and were distributed among the battalions and corps in boats ; and a boat-repairing party, under Lieutenant Kenney, R.E., arrived with repairing material. Its two boats' crews were from that moment almost incessantly at work.

While the work of organisation was going on, General Earle, with his own hand, drew up a series of rules for the movement of the troops in boats, for embarkations and disembarkations, for the bivouac, and for precautions on the march. He also designed special tactical formations for the march, with a view to rapidly passing from column into square, and square into column. These memoranda, together with others drawn up on the system of supply during the advance, and the medical arrangements for the troops, were circulated ; and during our stay at Hamdab, the troops were frequently practised by General Earle, in the tactical formations he had devised, over the very roughest ground.

CHAPTER IV.

HAMDAB—CONCENTRATION.

5th to 23d Jan. IT seemed at one time, during the earlier portion of our period of concentration at Hamdab, that the necessities of the desert column, on which so much depended, would seriously cripple us of the river route. Colonel Burnaby had been promised to us; and General Earle had hoped to have him for the command of the 6th Jan. mounted troops; but on the 6th January General Buller telegraphed, "I must steal Burnaby. I do not know who else is to 8th Jan. command Metemmeh." On the 8th General Buller still counted on sending us the West Kent Regiment, to take up posts on our 9th Jan. line of communications; but on the 9th the

first note of alarm to us was sounded.
" Every endeavour," General Buller wrote,
" will be made to complete the infantry of
your force up to 100 days' rations per man
before they start; but it is possible the
difficulties of transport may make it almost
impossible to do this within a reasonable
time.   It is desirable, therefore, for you to
consider whether it may not be possible
for you to advance, say two battalions of
infantry and a portion of your artillery
and mounted men, through the Monassir
country to Abu Hamed, and so open the
line of supply from Korosko."   In this
case, General Earle was to keep touch
of his rear battalions ; the Mudir's troops
assisting him to do this by occupying the
Monassir country; and he was reminded
that for the present his main objective was
the capture of Berber, and that for this
purpose he must concentrate his force.

To this minute General Earle replied 10th Jan.
that he should be prepared to advance with
two battalions and the mounted troops as

soon as he had two battalions of infantry
complete with 100 days' supply, together
with the portion of the transport company
allotted to his column, by which time he
hoped to have collected forage for the
animals and food for the Egyptian troops.
He considered all his small force of
mounted troops should accompany his advanced brigade, and he did not propose to
divide them, as opposition was to be expected to that brigade in the Monassir
country. He wished the Mudir's troops to
march parallel to us upon the right bank,
and to be ready to occupy the Monassir
country as soon as he had defeated the
Monassir tribe. He asked for two companies of a regiment from the line of communications to occupy Hamdab and a post
in the Monassir country; and in that case
anticipated no military difficulty for the
troops following the leading brigade, moving in half - battalions. General Earle
trusted that before he moved, his naval
boat, with a Gardner gun, his boat officers

and voyageurs, and boat-repairing party
might have reached his camp. He urged,
also, that his commissariat staff should be
promptly and considerably increased.

In reply General Earle was informed, on _{15th Jan.}
the 15th, that most of his requests were in
course of fulfilment; but that Lord Wolseley
did not approve his proposal to take with
him two companies of a line of communication regiment for the purpose of forming
posts on his line. He was instructed that
his force was to be a flying column; that
the General of communications would not
occupy the line behind us; and further, that
it was improbable the West Kent Regiment
could be rationed sufficiently in advance to
enable it to follow us up the river. Our,
at that time, very insufficient commissariat
staff could not yet be increased, because
there was no one at Korti to send to us.
Our land transport was on the 14th only
leaving Dongola; but Lord Wolseley was
anxious that our leading battalions should
advance at the very earliest moment to

occupy the Monassir country, and considered it not necessary that we should wait for our transport company, desiring General Earle to advance into the Monassir country, and there await the arrival of the transport.

At this time we had not a single baggage-camel, except the few belonging to the Egyptian Camel Corps and Artillery. To attempt an advance in boats into an enemy's country by an unknown river, without cavalry to scout on the banks, would have been an act of folly; and cavalry could not move without some transport. It is true that I had moved half a troop from Korti to Hamdab without any transport animals, by carrying their forage and equipment in the boats of the Staffords, and making the horses and the boats rendezvous together at night; but that was not a manœuvre to be attempted outside a peaceful country. Indeed it is well we did not attempt it, for after the first day's advance the boats had to take a channel which effectually separated them from all touch of the horses for two days.

There was another strong reason against our immediate advance. Our leading battalion, the Staffords, had been sent up with only thirty days' supplies, of which nearly twenty were already consumed. It had to fill up from the supplies of the Duke of Cornwall's Light Infantry, which we had halted at Abu Dom, and which, in its turn, had to fill up from the West Kent. This operation could not be completed till the 22d; and if we advanced without our full quantity of supplies, we should never be able to bring them up, as our completing our required amount depended absolutely on every infantry boat taking up its full 100 days per man in the boat. How important it seemed that we should not start without our full quantity can be judged from the fact that the same post which brought the above-named instructions to General Earle, also brought him instructions that, subject to the military necessities of the situation, he was to leave at Abu Hamed a garrison of 300 men, with sixty days' supply; and at Berber a garrison of 700 men with sixty days' supply, and also 40,000 complete rations; which, with 800 *ardebs* of dourra that we were to purchase at Berber, would be required for the use of a force to be sent from Berber to Suakim.

17th Jan.   General Earle, therefore, replied by telegraph to the Chief of the Staff on the 17th, that if the latter would send him forty baggage-camels, with saddles and drivers complete, at once, he could advance on the 23d, but not before, as the Staffords' supplies would not be complete sooner.

He also wrote at length, explaining the situation. He said in his memorandum: "As I am aware that there is a considerable force before us at Birti, as a prolonged halt in its immediate presence would be disadvantageous, and as I cannot inflict a severe defeat upon it without my small force of cavalry, I do not consider it ad-

visable to advance from this camp until I
can move with two battalions of infantry,
the Hussars and other mounted troops, to
the direct attack of the enemy's position."
He repeated the arguments stated above,
and his offer to advance on 23d if forty
camels were sent to him, and added: "I
must, however, point out, that by thus advancing without other land transport, I shall
be deprived of the means of making any
turning movement in the desert, which would
require a day's absence of the infantry from
their boats; and should difficult rapids
render portaging necessary, I shall be
without the means of carrying loads which
the transport allotted to me was specially
intended to provide."

On the 17th General Buller replied, "I
have not a camel or driver to send. They
are in the desert."

As regarded our power to carry out the
instructions for leaving supplies at Abu
Hamed and Berber, I went very carefully
into calculations; and the Chief of the Staff

was informed that, in the event of our starting, filled up with all the rations we could take, and receiving 50,000 rations at Korosko, we should, supposing us to be ready to leave Berber on 3d March, have at that date only twenty-eight days' supplies for the balance of our force (1800 men), after leaving the garrisons and supplies ordered at Abu Hamed and Berber. These calculations were accepted by the Chief of the Staff.

19th Jan.   On the 19th, the good news reached us that our transport under Captain Lea had reached Korti, would be completed to 350 serviceable camels, and would start on the 20th Jan. 20th; and on the 20th we were told that supplies to complete all our demands would leave at once in the steamer Nassif el Kheir, with the exception of certain quantities of biscuit, sugar, cocoa and milk for hospitals, salt, soap, and tobacco. General Buller's telegram ended: " The consignment by Nassif Kheir and Lea will complete all I can send you. You must be

thankful for small mercies, and go as quickly
as you can."

Colonel Butler arrived at Hamdab on
the 20th, and General Earle decided to
charge him with the duty of reconnoitring
for the advance of the force. He was to
move with the cavalry and camel corps
along the bank, cover the advance of and
select camping-grounds for the troops in
the boats; and he was to command the
advanced post whenever headquarters were
not present there.[1]

Lieutenant-Colonel Alleyne with a party 21st Jan.
of voyageurs arrived on the 21st. He was
charged with the direction of the advance
by river, and had as his assistants Captain
Orde, Rifle Brigade, Captain Lord Avonmore, Hampshire Regiment, and Lieutenant Peel, 2d Life Guards, all by this time
thoroughly experienced in boat-work on
the Nile.

---

[1] At Colonel Butler's request, Major Martin, R.A., and
Lieutenant Pirie, 2d Life Guards, were attached to him as
staff officers.

Captain Courtney, R.E., and Captain Hon. F. Colborne, Royal Irish Rifles, arrived for the purpose of surveying the river as we advanced.

The headquarters of the 1st battalion Royal Highlanders (Black Watch) arrived in our camp on the 13th, and the battalion was completed in the course of the next few days.

21st to 23d Jan.

The headquarters of the 1st battalion Gordon Highlanders arrived on the 21st, but the battalion was still incomplete on the 24th. One company had been left to garrison Halfa; and one company, with the Lieutenant-Colonel second in command, was still far behind.

The 2d battalion Duke of Cornwall's Light Infantry, after handing over its supplies to the Staffords at Abu Dom, waited there to complete its own supplies from convoys sent up from Korti. Its first half-battalion reached Hamdab on the 23d; its headquarters and remaining half on the 24th.

The camel battery marched from Abu Dom to Hamdab on the 22d, joining the camel corps there.

After placing great difficulties in the way, the Mudir of Dongola had consented to his troops advancing into the Monassir country by the right bank. I do not propose to enter into any detail of their composition, or into the story of their march. It is sufficient here to state that, after having succeeded in taking over the Vakeel's fort at Abu Dom for the use of the two companies of the Essex Regiment, which arrived there as garrison on the 23d, Colvile succeeded in getting the Mudir's troops crossed over to the right bank at Merawi on the 21st and 22d. On the 23d, to the number of 310, they made a short march out from Merawi, complete, Colvile informed us, with transport (camels and donkeys) and ammunition (120 rounds per man), but without riding-camels for scouting. They had also a brass gun, which they used to fire off at night. The

E

Vakeel accompanied them, saying it was necessary he should do so, to prevent ill-treatment of friendly natives. Before starting, he telegraphed to the Mudir to say that, "with God's help, he hoped to collect some taxes."

The situation in the Soudan, as known to us at this time, was as follows. Herbert Stewart, having established a post at Gakdul, had returned to Korti, had again advanced to and beyond Gakdul, and had fought the action of Abu Klea. Our knowledge of the details of that fight was very limited; but we could read between the lines of the telegrams, and could tell that Stewart had met with a very determined resistance, and that somehow the enemy had got inside the square. We were told that Stewart was continuing his advance on Metemmeh.

A messenger from Gordon, who had left for Khartoum on 18th December, had returned to Korti on 11th January; but unfortunately, on his way back his letters had been taken from him, and he had been so severely beaten he could recollect nothing. Thus our latest news from Khartoum was still the few words—" All well, 14th December," and the verbal message mentioned in the first chapter.

From Berber we had news as late as the 23d December. All was then quiet there. There were very few soldiers in the town; they were spread about in the surrounding villages—the Egyptian soldiers working as slaves at the *sakyehs*. The town was said to be surrounded by an intrenchment; and there were some guns, varying in the statements from three to six in number, on the left bank of the river at Robush or Masseed, the village opposite Berber. Mohammed el Kheir, the Mahdi's Emir of Berber, had applied to the Mahdi for reinforcements and guns, but had met with a refusal to send them.

From Abu Hamed we had news as late as the 3d January. The *sakyehs* between Berber and Abu Hamed were then at work.

Abu Hegel, chief of the Robatab, was at
his own village. Sheikhs Hassan Wad Hag
Said and Ali Basha were at Abu Hamed—
having replaced two sheikhs who had been
recalled, because they had not reported a
reconnaissance to near Abu Hamed made
by Major Rundle and Sheikh Saleh Bey in
November.

Our latest news from Birti was of the
18th January; but we had spies there who
were to inform us of any serious change in
the situation. Suleiman Wad Gamr had
returned from Berber, but had gone to Salamat to meet Abdul Majid Wad Abu Lekalik, who had arrived from Berber with
reinforcements at least a thousand strong,
and he was remaining at Salamat to bring
up more reinforcements. Lekalik, as we
shall hereafter call him, was on the 18th
at Birti with 1500 dervishes and the Monassir and Robatab, and had been placed by
the Emir of Berber in command of all the
troops there. He was said to have been
anxious to advance to fight us, but Sulei-

man had urged remaining at Birti; and now that Lekalik had agreed to remaining at Birti, Suleiman wanted to retire to the Shukook Pass. Moussa Wad Abu Hegel was still at Birti, and said to be full of fight.

To sum up the state of the information obtained through our intelligence department up to 23d January: All was well at Khartoum on 14th December; Stewart had had a hard fight, and was advancing on Metemmeh on 18th January; Berber was quiet, and not strongly defended, on 23d December; Abu Hamed had a small garrison and no defences on 3d January; a force about 3000 strong was in front of us at Birti—consisting of Berberines, Monassir, and Robatab, about 500 of them having rifles—and its commander meant fighting. Buller had told us that, from various accounts of Stewart's fight, he found that "these Arabs do charge home, and very quickly," and had advised us "not to let them get a run at us unless we were in square."

Our orders were to advance through the
Monassir country, take and garrison Abu
Hamed, receive a convoy from Korosko,
and advance on Berber. When near Berber—within twenty miles—we were to fire
a gun and two rockets every night at twelve.
The desert column was to have steamers
and men six or eight miles above Berber,
and would answer our signal, and the steamers would then reconnoitre and assist our
attack. We knew that Rundle had 700
camels ready to march from Korosko, and
we had arranged signals to let him know
of our proximity to Abu Hamed; and we
telegraphed to Cairo asking that our letters
and papers by the mail leaving Cairo 22d
should be sent to Korosko to await the
departure of this convoy. We also arranged for supplies of such vitally necessary material as paint for the boats and
shoes for the horses being sent by the same
route.

22d Jan.   On the 22d Colonel Butler reconnoitred
to Ooli island, and selected a site for a

camp. He reported the river free from obstacles to that point. The natives had fled between Kulgeili and Ooli, but at the latter place some were remaining.

On the 23d our transport, about 330 23d Jan. camels, under Captain Lea, arrived at Hamdab. Arrangements were at once made for handing over regimental transport to the Hussars, the necessary transport to headquarters, and for mounting staff officers, who had been sent up to the column without any sort of mount; and then orders for the advance on the following day were issued.

Colonel Hammill, of the Gordon Highlanders, was left in command at Hamdab, with orders to send on the Cornwalls by half-battalions on 25th and 26th, with two sections of the field-hospital. On the 26th he was to send on the Egyptian battery and the transport company under escort of a portion of the camel corps, left behind for this purpose, the whole under command of Major Wodehouse, R.A. He was himself to follow with his own battalion and two sections of field - hospital, as soon as his battalion was concentrated, having previously sent down to Abu Dom any superfluous stores remaining at Hamdab, and disestablished the telegraph.

General Buller, in asking me to send him a state of our force before actually starting, had said to me : " I know you have been handicapped; but now the force is completed, I mention that I know Lord Wolseley attaches great importance to your making as rapid an advance as possible;" and had asked me for the probable date of our arrival at Abu Hamed. I replied : "We start to-morrow. It is impossible to predict the date of reaching Abu Hamed. It must depend on nature of river and opposition of enemy, both unknown quantities."

CHAPTER V.

BEFORE General Earle left Korti, Lord
Wolseley gave him some dates of probable
moves, which he entered in his pocket-
book. The first of these was, " Leave
Hamdab, 24th January." We were punc-
tual to our time. On the morning of the 24th Jan.
24th the advance commenced at 7 A.M.
The Hussars and half the camel corps
marched at seven, their baggage and headquarter baggage following at 10 o'clock
under an escort of mounted troops. Two
companies of the Staffordshire, with Lieut.-
Colonel Alleyne and the other boat officers,
moved off by river at seven, followed by

the boats of the Royal Engineers, and then
the remainder of the battalion.   The Black
Watch followed at eight; the boat-repairing party, the senior medical officer, half the
field-hospital, two headquarter boats, and
three guard boats manned by Gordon
Highlanders, moving between the half-
battalions of the Black Watch.   The masts
of all whalers were lowered before starting,
as we were about to commence a long journey against the prevailing north wind.

Headquarters marched about 11 A.M.
Before starting we telegraphed to Korti:
" Just off; all going as well as possible;
troops in high spirits, longing for a fight;
no sick."   As we rode along the bank we
saw many boats in difficulties.   The channel was full of sunken rocks; and nine boats
had to be unloaded, hauled up, and repaired
either by their own crews or the boat-
repairing party.   The last boats did not
arrive opposite Ooli island, about eight
miles from Hamdab, till 7 P.M.; but by half-
past 7 we were all in bivouac.   The

anchorage on the left bank being scanty, the
Black Watch bivouacked on the right bank
opposite. The position for the bivouac of
the Staffords and mounted troops was on
a high Nile island—that is to say, on land
which, though now connected with the mainland, would at high Nile be entirely separated
from it by a wide deep channel, now only
partially full and crossed by a causeway.

On the arrival of the leading boats, the
mounted troops reconnoitred along the left
bank, a short distance beyond Kabour, and
found the country deserted. Two of the
boat officers reconnoitred by river. The
result of the combined reports, and of native information, was that the channel along
the left bank was impracticable for boats;
and it was decided that the channel on the
right bank, on the far side of Great Ooli
island, must be used. It was found that
it could be reached from the left bank
channel by a narrow dyke between Great
Ooli island and another small island just
opposite the camp of the Staffords.

And now commenced our first military
difficulty, necessitating the first of those
moves in the game of chess which we subsequently had to play. The infantry was
about to be effectually separated from the
mounted troops. Any boats sent into the
rapids in the right-bank channel would be
as completely separated from us for the
time being as if they were a hundred miles
away. A force of 3000 of the enemy was
known to be within eighteen miles of us;
and in the rocky and difficult country into
which we had now entered, every move
must be made with caution. If there was
one thing more important than another, it
was that we should avoid the smallest
chance of being surprised. It would not
do to send a small force of 60 Hussars and
40 Egyptian Camel Corps to bivouac by
themselves in advance on the left bank.
Yet the head of the rapid through which
the troops were about to pass must be held,
and cavalry must scout well to its front.
It was therefore decided to march half a

battalion of the Black Watch to the neighbourhood of Kabour to form a post there, with the cavalry and camel corps at a point where the Staffords, who were to be sent into the right - bank channel, would again emerge into the main stream at the head of Suffi island.

About 7 P.M. we got into heliographic communication with Colvile, who had, with the Mudir's troops, reached Ummerikh, on the right bank opposite our bivouac. We sent over a signaller to relieve one of his who had been touched by the sun, and at the same time ordered him to advance the following day on the right bank to the head of the rapid (known as Edermih cataract) into which we were about to launch the Staffords.

Information as to the channel between Hamdab and our present bivouac was sent back to Hamdab, for the use of the troops who were to follow, and the messenger took back our report of progress for the Chief of the Staff.

On the morning of the 25th, Colonel

Butler moved off with the mounted troops, and selected a strong position for the advanced post on a small rocky high Nile island, just above the head of Suffi island; and the half-battalion Black Watch arrived there at 10 o'clock. The Staffords had moved into the dike leading to the right-bank channel at 6.45 A.M., and soon after 8 o'clock their last boat was lost to view. Half the battalion Black Watch remained at Ooli bivouac, where, in the course of the day, they were joined by the leading half-battalion of the Duke of Cornwall's Light Infantry.

General Earle with his staff rode to the advanced post, arriving there about 11 A.M. Communication by heliograph was at once established with the Ooli bivouac, and about the same time the Mudir's troops arrived at Mushra el Abiad on the opposite bank, and Colvile established his heliograph there.

We then rode up the river as far as Kabenat, about three miles beyond Kabour. Here we found a strong fort, with walls eight to twelve feet thick built of loose

stones, and capable of holding a garrison
of 500 men, on the top of a high detached
hill, completely commanding the river and
bank; and a similar fort opposite on the
right bank, with swift and difficult water
flowing between. Who built these forts?
From what period do they date? There is
a vague tradition among the Soudanese that
they were built by some Christian power
some centuries ago, and I am satisfied these
forts are of comparatively modern date.
Ascending to the fort, we obtained an extended view, and were shortly joined by
Colonel Butler, who told us he had reconnoitred to the cataract of Kab el Abd, five
miles further on. He reported the country
clear and fairly open, and the water fairly
clear up to Kab el Abd, the cataract there
being like the big gate of Semneh. All the
country beyond Ooli camp was deserted.

We returned to Kabour post, and about
4 P.M. got into communication by heliograph
with Colonel Alleyne on Suffi island.
He told us three complete companies were

through the cataract; so he was ordered to send on two companies to relieve the half-battalion Black Watch, which Colonel Butler was ordered to send back to Ooli as soon as relieved. Colvile was directed to keep the Mudir's troops halted till further orders. Instructions were sent back to Hamdab to detain the artillery and transport there till further orders, and to send two officers of the Gordon Highlanders to view the river as far as Kabenat, in order to expedite the advance of the battalion later on. General Earle and staff then returned to the Ooli bivouac.

Two companies of the Staffords reached the Kabour advanced post shortly after dark; but as the pickets of the Black Watch were posted, Colonel Butler did not relieve them, and the half-battalion did not return to Ooli till the following morning.

26th Jan. At the usual hour on the 26th (6.45 A.M.), the half-battalion Black Watch at Ooli, with one boat of repairing party, and field-hospital, moved off into the Edermih cataract, piloted by a boat officer sent back for the purpose, and followed by the second half-battalion, as soon as it arrived from Kabour. The second half-battalion of the Cornwalls arrived at Ooli.

General Earle and his staff again rode to Kabour. The Staffords completed the passage of the cataract, and concentrated at the advanced post. In the afternoon we embarked in a whaler and crossed to the Mudir's camp, where General Earle inspected the Mudir's troops under Achmet Effendi. The Vakeel was living in a tent, with carpets and cushions—a great contrast to our primitive open-air bivouac. Coffee was served, the situation was discussed, and we then dropped down in our boat to the head of Suffi island, where we met Colonel Alleyne, and walked with him to the cataract. The leading wing of the Black Watch was passing through, and the rear wing was closing up at the foot of the rapid. The cataract (Edermih) was a very troublesome one. In the first place, two

F

small shoots or rapids had to be tracked up ;
then came three-quarters of a mile of swift
broken rapids, with four shoots or rushes of
water, the last of which was like the great
gate of Semneh. Arms, ammunition, and
accoutrements had to be portaged for three-
quarters of a mile, and the crews of three
boats had to be employed to haul one boat
through. Alleyne thought it was as bad
water as any on the river.

We returned to Kabour, and thence to
Ooli, leaving orders with Colonel Butler to
advance with the Staffords and as many
of the Black Watch as possible to Kab el
Abd next day. Only two companies of the
Black Watch reached Kabour that night.

Orders were sent to Colonel Hammill at
Hamdab for the artillery and transport to
march with their escort on the 28th. Colvile was instructed to move in the morning
with the Mudir's troops, and take up a position opposite Kab el Abd. Meanwhile
he was to urge the Vakeel to keep his
troops in hand, as they had been setting fire

to huts, and we were in a theoretically friendly country. The Cornwalls were ordered to advance into the Edermih cataract in the morning.

In the night one of our spies returned from Birti. He brought word that on Saturday the 24th there were at Birti some 2500 men, under five chiefs, of whom the most prominent were Lekalik, Suleiman Wad Gamr, and Moussa Wad Abu Hegel. He told us it was their intention to attack us when our boats were separated in the cataract of Kab el Abd, or beyond it, and that they meant to attack in the early morning, when it was cold.

Colonel Butler was then further instructed to push on to the foot of Kab el Abd, and concentrate the two leading battalions there. He was to reconnoitre with the mounted troops till he should get touch of the enemy, endeavouring to ascertain his strength and position, and falling back upon the infantry; and Colvile was directed to advance his troops only as far as Shebabit, and to push

a reconnaissance on the right bank as nearly opposite to Birti as he could reach, endeavouring to ascertain the enemy's strength
and position there.

27th Jan.   On the 27th the Cornwalls advanced into
the Edermih cataract, and the Staffords and
Black Watch concentrated about a mile
short of Kab el Abd cataract, where headquarters joined them. A strong position
was taken up here, and a zareeba made.
It was ascertained that the great gate of
the cataract could be avoided by tracking
up the opposite bank.

Meanwhile the mounted troops advanced,
and some two and a half miles beyond the
cataract sighted about 120 of the enemy on
foot, with seven or eight horsemen, near the
tomb of a sheikh at Warag. Shots were
exchanged at about a thousand yards, and
the enemy retiring, a further advance was
made. Colonel Butler reported on return
to camp that about two miles above the
great gate of Kab el Abd there commenced
two miles of bad rapid water.

The news of the river was bad. We seemed to have entered upon a succession of troublesome rapids. The land, too, was as bad as it could well be—nothing but black rocks and sand everywhere; scarcely a scrap of cultivation visible. But the news that the cavalry had really exchanged shots with the enemy cheered us, and there were tangible results in the shape of four camels, six oxen, and sixty sheep, captured by Marriott's camel corps. General Earle, telegraphing that night, reported, " Troops in excellent spirits, and only seven slight cases of sickness in whole force."

Meanwhile Colvile had not let the grass grow under his feet. No sooner had he reached Shebabit than, mounting ten of the Mudir's men on ten of his best baggage-camels, he pushed on with them fourteen miles to Hush el Jeruf, the village right opposite Birti, whence he obtained a good view of the enemy's camp. He described it to us as situated on a gentle slope, running down from a low range of hills to the

river, the ground being broken and rocky,
and the camp commanded on all sides.
Owing to the nature of the ground it was
difficult to see distinctly, but his impression
was that there were not more than 1000
of the enemy. Three tents were visible.
About 300 of the enemy had collected on
a rise in the ground, and watched his party.

On his return over a succession of what
at high Nile would be islands, but which
had now a dry channel between them and
the mainland, he met with no opposition,
but was followed by a small body of horse
and foot. He learned that several desertions had taken place from among the
enemy.

He described the population on the right
bank as remaining at work on its *sakyehs*,
and presenting, therefore, a very different
appearance to that of the barren deserted
waste through which we were passing on
the left bank.

That evening we received through Korti
a long telegram from Colonel Rundle at

Korosko, giving details of the tribes who, according to the report of his sheikhs, were gathered to oppose us at Birti.   It wound up thus : " I can get none of the sheikhs to go below 10,000 as the force in front. of General Earle.   They have no doubt now of their intention to fight."

Orders were issued for the advance to commence at the usual hour in the morning; and Colvile was directed to cover the advance of the boats on the right bank, and endeavour to communicate with our signallers on Mishami ridge.

CHAPTER VI.

KAB EL ABD TO GAMRA—RETREAT OF THE
ENEMY.

28th Jan. EARLY on the 28th the infantry advanced
in their boats. The Staffords and Black
Watch passed through the Kab el Abd
cataract, with damage to two boats of the
Black Watch, and reached a point in the
rapids about two miles distant from their
camp of the previous night, immediately
opposite the foot of Kandi island. The
anchorage on the left bank was apparently
insufficient for two battalions, and the Black
Watch bivouacked on Kandi island—the
Staffords occupying a semicircular position,
which was covered by a zareeba, with outposts and sentries placed on a bastion-like
hill in front of the camp. It was a most

unsatisfactory military position; but we were on this occasion, as on others, compelled to bivouac on sites badly suited for defence, as we were restricted in the choice of sites by the limit of distance the boats could travel, and the necessity for bivouacking where there was anchorage. This was a wind-swept, sun-baked, dusty spot, without shade by day or shelter by night, at the extremity of a ridge of forbidding black rocks known as Mishami ridge.

Meanwhile the Cornwalls completed the passage of the Edermih cataract, begun on the previous day, and reached the foot of Kab el Abd, where we had bivouacked the previous night.

Our mounted troops reconnoitred as far as Rahami cataract, seven or eight miles to the front; and Colonel Butler reported no signs of the enemy. It would, he considered, be possible to push a battalion through the rapids immediately in front of us by nightfall on the 29th, but it would be necessary to portage arms and ammunition.

Colvile had vainly tried to find a position on the right bank opposite us; but the rocky nature of the ground, and the numerous islands intervening between the right and left bank, made it impossible. He, however, found a safe camping-ground on Umkumtata island nearly opposite Gamra, about three miles above our camp at Mishami ridge, all the channels between the islands themselves, and between the islands and the right bank, being sufficiently dry to admit of their being crossed by the Mudir's troops.

Our artillery and transport, with an escort of half Major Marriott's Egyptian Camel Corps, marched from Hamdab, and took up a position, surrounded by a zareeba, on some open ground about a mile in our rear, where there was a certain amount of forage and a good watering-place for the camels.

29th Jan. At 6.45 on the 29th, six companies of the Black Watch marched to Warag, and took up a position on fairly open ground at the head of the rapid ; while the mounted troops pushed on, with orders from General Earle that they were to push home to Birti and bring back information as to the enemy's strength. The Cornwalls passed through the Kab el Abd cataract, and arrived at Mishami ridge, when we at once proceeded to form a zareeba on a horse-shoe-topped hill, which we held at night with the Cornwalls and half the Black Watch.

The Staffords entered the Umhaboah rapid at the same early hour. It proved to be the worst piece of water yet encountered, and it was with great difficulty and labour that four companies succeeded in working their way to Warag by sunset. Meanwhile the Black Watch had been forming a zareeba; and as soon as the half-battalion of the Staffords reached it, two companies of the Black Watch marched back to Mishami ridge, leaving half a battalion at Warag with the Staffords. The other wing of the Staffords bivouacked together in a zareeba about half-way through the rapid.

In the course of the morning a report
was received from Colonel Colvile that a
spy had returned from Birti with news that
reinforcements from Berber, which would
bring the Birti force up to 5000 men, had
left Salamat on the 27th, and were to
reach Birti on the 29th. Part of this force
was said to be advancing on the right bank;
and as General Earle did not wish Colonel
Colvile and the Mudir's troops to run any
risk of being attacked by superior force in
an isolated position, he directed Colvile
to fall back to the end of Kandi island,
opposite Mishami ridge. Colvile came
himself with a few men, and was brought
over to our camp in a boat; but the Vakeel
protested against falling back, as it would
tire his men, and he could not find anywhere
on the islands so good and open a position
as the one he was in. As the Mudir's troops
seemed to be free from anxiety as to their
position, General Earle did not press his
order for their return.

Orders were sent back to Hamdab di-

recting the Gordon Highlanders to move
without fail on the 30th; and a boat officer
who had been twice through Edermih
cataract and once through Kab el Abd,
was sent to pilot them from Ooli.

On Colonel Butler's return at night, we
learnt the result of his reconnaissance. He
had pushed to within a mile of Birti, and
had found the hills approaching close to the
river, leaving only a narrow space for the
road, which was rough, stony, and broken.
He had come in sight of a body of the
enemy about 700 to 800 yards distant, apparently advancing, and had retired from
the broken ground, and taken up a position. Slade had ascended a hill from
which he had looked down on the enemy's
camp, and had seen a body of them, whose
number he estimated at 2000, parading with
the apparent object of advancing. Marriott
on the right had fallen in with a scouting-
party of the enemy, and had exchanged
shots, having one camel killed. He had
worked down a wady to the right, from

which he had seen three camps of the
enemy.

News reached us to-day that Herbert
Stewart had advanced on the 18th, and had
had a second fight on the 19th. We were
told that the enemy did not charge home so
well as on the 17th, and that our men's
steady volleys had been too much for them;
but that they shot well with their Remingtons. Our troops, we learnt, were strongly
intrenched at Goubat, two miles south of
Metemmeh, which was still held by the
enemy. Four of Gordon's steamers were
co-operating with us, of which two had
started on the 24th for Khartoum with
Sir C. Wilson and a small detachment of
the Sussex Regiment. Herbert Stewart,
we were told, was severely wounded, but
was progressing satisfactorily, and great
hopes were entertained of his recovery.
Talbot with a large convoy had reached
Gakdul from Goubat. Half the Royal Irish
had left Korti on the 28th; the remainder
and West Kent were to follow. Wilson

reported large reinforcements marching from Berber to Metemmeh. General Buller was going to take command, and told us that "if Khartoum is sufficiently provisioned, we don't mean to do anything until you join us."

Our situation was aggravating. The desert column already on the Nile above Metemmeh, and proposing to wait there till we could join them; the enemy in force in our front ten miles away; and our troops scattered along these terrible rapids, which seemed to grow more and more difficult with each mile of our advance. There was nothing for it but to push on, and concentrate a sufficient force within striking distance of the enemy, who was apparently resolved to hold his ground at Birti.

I for one slept lightly that night. It was bitterly cold, and there was no escaping the wind. A full moon, which we hoped was to light us to victory at Birti, was shining. More than once I walked round the zareeba, where our sentries were standing motion-

less, looking out over the rocks and ravines
around.   At last I was sleeping soundly,
when I was awakened by the field-officer of
the Black Watch on duty, who told me that
a native dressed in white had crept up,
leading a horse, to within a few yards of
the zareeba, had looked down upon our
cavalry below, and had then made off again.
Did it portend an early attack?   If so, we
were ready at any moment.   The first note
of alarm by one of our sentries would have
brought all our men, armed and accoutred,
to their feet, and have lined the zareeba
with a circle of bayonets, and of rifles ready
to sweep the surrounding space with their
fire.   Should we hear firing from either of
our smaller advanced posts, and have to
march to their assistance; or was it only
a bold spy, come to learn our strength and
dispositions for defence?

Nothing came to disturb us further.
30th Jan.   *Réveillé* sounded at five; and the troops
stood to their arms as usual.   Our cavalry
patrols went out, and to them at once

surrendered himself the gentleman who had visited us the night before. His story was as follows : He had been an Egyptian soldier, one of the garrison of Berber, when that place was taken by the Mahdi; he had been made to join the Mahdi's troops; he had been one of the force which marched from Berber to Birti under Lekalik, and had been made to take command of a body of riflemen there, commanding outposts at night, and visiting the troops by day. He said that on the previous night he had deserted, bringing with him a horse, the property of Moussa Wad Abu Hegel, and his rifle and ammunition. He told us that the force at Birti consisted of 5000 Monassir, 4000 Robatab, and 6000 Bisharin and Berberines; but that there were only 300 rifles, and thirty rounds of ammunition per rifle. He said that the gun from Stewart's steamer was there, but spiked and without ammunition. Lekalik had first seen our scouts on the 25th; he had then intended occupying Mishami ridge, but

found it held by us on the 28th. The
enemy had made a stone parapet, facing
the road and river at Birti, but no other
defences ; and they intended standing
there, though the Robatab were deserting.
Lekalik and Moussa had followed our
retiring scouts yesterday on horseback ; and
drums were beating all evening. Our
friend told us that Lekalik had received a
letter from Berber telling him there had
been a great fight at Metemmeh.

There was nothing in this information to
alter the dispositions made for the day.
Half a battalion of the Cornwalls marched
to Warag, and relieved the wing of the
Black Watch there. The Staffords continued their advance through the cataract,
and concentrated at Warag, where also half
a battalion of the Black Watch arrived in
its boats. The other wing of the Black
Watch, after its return to Mishami, entered
the Umhaboah cataract, but did not get
through, bivouacking where half the Staffords had bivouacked on the previous

night. The Cornwalls remained at Mishami ridge. Headquarters and the mounted
troops moved to Warag. Cavalry had a
quiet day, vedettes out, and nothing of
importance occurred.

Above Warag there still lay two miles of
bad rapid water to Gamra, where there was
excellent anchorage and camping-ground.
Gamra was about seven miles from Birti,
and General Earle decided to concentrate
three battalions, the mounted troops, and
artillery there; and to make it the point
from which he would march to attack the
enemy, leaving his boats and transport
covered by a strong detachment in a good
zareeba, with clear field of fire. Accordingly
on the 31st he marched the Staffords by 31st Jan.
land to Gamra, covered by the mounted
troops. On arrival they prepared the
ground, and made a zareeba for the Black
Watch, who advanced in boats, being so
much retarded by the difficult water that
they did not succeed in concentrating at
Gamra till 7 P.M., when the Staffords

marched back to Warag. The Cornwalls, in the meantime, entered the Umhaboah cataract; six companies reached Warag, and two bivouacked in rear. Their reserve ammunition was carried on camels to Gamra.

Colonel Butler's report of the direct road along the river to the enemy's camp did not seem to favour a direct attack. We should apparently have to force our way through a gorge between rocks and river, commanded by hills on our right; and should, on emerging, find ourselves faced by the enemy's stone parapet, of which the deserter had told us. It was therefore very desirable, from tactical as well as strategical reasons, to find a way by which we could outflank the position; and I was sent by General Earle to ascertain if such a way was to be found. Accompanied by Colonel Butler, Colonel Colvile, Major Slade, and the deserter from Birti, I reconnoitred with the mounted troops to the south-east into the desert; and ascending a high detached hill about six miles from our camp, and

four and a half miles from Birti, discovered that the low hills which enclosed the
position of Birti formed a semicircle, with
its flanks on the river; that immediately
behind the hills there ran, straight from
the hill on which we were, a broad *khor*
or wady,—a dry sandy watercourse, which
struck the river beyond the enemy's camp,
and at the end of which we could see the
palm-trees on the river-bank that marked
—so our deserter said—the site of Suleiman
Wad Gamr's abode. It was evident that
from this wady there were branches leading
straight into the enemy's camp, and the
deserter assured us it was so. Here then
was our line of attack clearly marked out,
and the more satisfactorily that the *khor*
could be reached from the camp at Gamra
without passing over more than about two
miles of broken ground.

It struck us at the time as singular that
we saw no signs of the enemy's presence,
—not a man on the look-out, not a beast
grazing on the shrubs and coarse grass of

the wady; and I should have pushed our reconnaissance along the wady, were it not that, feeling sure General Earle would adopt this line of attack, I did not like to show our hand. Up to this time the enemy evidently considered us only capable of moving along the river-bank, and it would be dangerous to disabuse their minds too soon.

On our return to camp in the evening, Slade proceeded to examine at length a deserter who had come into our camp in the morning, but whom he had only cursorily questioned before our start to reconnoitre. From this man he learnt that on the previous day—a report having been received at Birti that the English would attack from the desert side, and that the Turks (Mudir's troops) would advance on the right bank—a council of war had been held, at which it was decided to retire. The troops had broken up at sunset, and marched (about 1500 in number) towards Salamat, with the intention, this deserter said, of going to the Shukook pass. So, if this were true, Birti was empty at the very time we were reconnoitring for the best way to attack it.

Before starting with me in the morning, Colvile had received a letter from the Vakeel. I must preface what is coming by saying that the Vakeel, when at Korti at New Year, had been promised a very handsome reward if he were instrumental in catching Suleiman Wad Gamr and the blind man, and was very eager to earn it. His letter now was to the effect that last night (30th), Omar, Suleiman's uncle, had come in, and asked the Vakeel to promise him for the remainder of his tribe and Suleiman, that nobody would hurt them. The Vakeel had promised that no harm should happen to them or to Suleiman, whereupon Omar had gone back to bring them. "We shall get them by these means," said the Vakeel, "and then we can do what we like." The Vakeel was in high spirits over this joyful news, which must have been rather damped by Colonel

Colvile's reply : " We will treat Omar and his brothers well if they come in ; but the only promise we can make to Suleiman Wad Gamr and Colonel Stewart's murderers is, that we will hang them if we catch them."   .

Colvile, as soon as he returned to our camp, crossed over and saw the Vakeel, reminded him of his repeated instructions to make no terms with Suleiman Wad Gamr, and said his proposal could not be for a moment entertained. To this he replied that the only way we could get through our difficulties was by leading Suleiman to believe we were his friends, and killing him afterwards. On Colvile refusing to listen to such a proposal, the Vakeel handed him a letter of remonstrance, saying that if we could bring in Suleiman, the tribes before us would be scattered; if not, we should have great trouble. Colvile then returned to our camp, and in the course of the evening received another letter from the Vakeel,

saying that Omar and Abu Bekr, Suleiman's
uncles, had come into his camp as friends,
asserting that they had sent Lekalik and
Moussa, with their people, away out of their
country, and that they held their own people
to be with the Government. This was
rather amusing, considering that neither
Omar nor Abu Bekr had any authority
over the Monassir, and that Lekalik and
Moussa had only retired the night before
to seek a better position in the Shukook
pass.

Colvile was directed to inform the Vakeel immediately that General Earle distinctly refused to acknowledge, and repu-
diated, any promises made to Suleiman
Wad Gamr; and that General Earle had
been sent here to punish Suleiman and the
other murderers of Colonel Stewart and the
English and French Consuls, and to punish
those who had made themselves accomplices in the murder by not bringing in
Suleiman as a prisoner. Colvile was further instructed to proceed at an early hour

on the 1st to the Vakeel's camp, and bring him over to see General Earle, bringing over at the same time Omar and Abu Bekr.

Colonel Butler was directed to reconnoitre to Birti with the mounted troops as early as possible in the morning of the 1st; half a battalion of the Black Watch was directed to march towards Birti in support of his reconnaissance; and all troops in rear of Gamra were ordered to advance by boat.

CHAPTER VII.

BIRTI—HALT, AND ADVANCE OF THE ENEMY.

AT the usual early hour on the 1st February, 1st Feb.
the troops moved as ordered. Colonel
Butler entered Birti, and found it deserted;
his scouts, pushing three miles farther, found
traces of the enemy's retreat. As soon as
his report arrived, the wing of the Black
Watch, which had been pushed on in support, was ordered back; and as the leading
Staffords arrived at Gamra, the other wing
of the Black Watch was pushed on into the
Rahami cataract, and a wing of the Cornwalls was ordered on into the rapids to
follow the Staffords. The artillery and
convoy were ordered up from their position
in rear of Mishami to Gamra.

Colonel Colvile brought over the Vakeel into our camp. Gaudet seemed incapable of believing we were so stupid as to be in earnest in refusing to capture Suleiman by promises of safety, with a view to putting him to death subsequently; but at last our dull obstinacy overcame him, and he believed. He still, however, had some hopes of catching Suleiman through the agency of Omar and Abu Bekr, and accordingly they were allowed to return to his camp, where Colvile also returned. Later in the day, however, he learned that Suleiman had fled beyond recall. He then threw up his hand in disgust, and withdrew his opposition to our issuing the proclamation offering rewards for the apprehension of Suleiman and the blind man, which he had hitherto declared would remove the last hope of capturing either of them.

His interview with the Vakeel ended, General Earle rode on to the advanced post of the Black Watch, and as soon as he received Colonel Butler's report that

Birti was deserted, he rode on there. He discovered the boat of Colonel Stewart's steamer on the shore, and there came running to him a man who announced himself to be Hassain, the stoker of the ill-fated steamer. Hassain gave the story of the wreck and the murder in detail. It differed little from the accounts so well known, and so often published; but it fixed the date of the murder as Thursday, 18th September, and it more directly connected Suleiman with the murder than any account we had yet heard. He had made his way down the river after the murder, had been taken prisoner, and kept safe by Omar, Suleiman's uncle, who had used him as a slave. We were anxious to keep him with us, that he might identify the site of the murder on our reaching Hebbeh; but he was eager to return to his home in Upper Egypt, and soon made his escape.

Our mounted troops fell back to Gamra, and that night we bivouacked as under :—

Half the Black Watch in advance of
Gamra in the Rahami cataract.

Headquarters, mounted troops, Staffords,
half the Black Watch, artillery, and convoy
at Gamra.

Half the Cornwalls at Warag, and half
in the Umhaboah cataract between Warag
and Mishami.

The Gordons were through the Edermih
cataract; and Captain Orde, the boat officer
sent to pilot them, reported that cataract
far worse than when he had passed it
before, owing to the considerable fall of
the river.

In reading through the rough diary of
our daily proceedings, I am struck by the
frequency of the expression applied to the
rapids: "The worst yet encountered," or
"the most difficult yet met with." The
fact is, that from Ooli to Birti the river was
but a succession of rapids as bad as it was
possible for the boats to pass. If there
was one part worse than another, it was
the series of rapids along the left bank

between Gamra and Birti, known as the Rahami cataract. Into this half the Black Watch had already penetrated; and the remaining wing was sent forward early on the 2d February. 2d Feb.

All our boat officers were suffering in health from constant exposure to the sun, severe physical fatigue, and the incessant strain upon their energies. There was danger of their breaking down; and accordingly, two additional officers were selected and appointed to act as boat officers —Lieutenant Morris, D.C.L.I., and Lieutenant Livingstone of the Black Watch. The rapids immediately before us proved fully sufficient to tax their powers to the utmost.

General Earle considered it important to occupy Birti at once; and as the news of the enemy's movements justified him in pushing forward the mounted troops alone, Colonel Butler was sent on with the Hussars and camel corps to form a zareeba and hold it. Having formed a zareeba, he reconnoitred five miles in advance, and came upon some baggage and provisions abandoned by the enemy. He saw no inhabitants. The river was smooth, resembling a Scotch loch; the country along the shore exceedingly rough, with rocks coming down to near the river.

A refugee from the rebel camp reported that the rebels had halted a day at the entrance to the Shukook pass, but when they heard that the English were in Birti they had retired farther. He had heard that Lekalik and Suleiman were going to Berber, and Moussa to the Robatab country. There had been many desertions since Birti was abandoned, and Suleiman, who had seen the proclamation offering a reward for his capture, was reported to be in great alarm. A report from Colonel Colvile, however, said that the information brought to the Vakeel was to the effect that the rebels were halted, and were holding the Shukook pass.

The leading wing of the Black Watch

was, early in the day, engaged in overcoming a most serious succession of bad
rushes of water; and its progress was very
slow. Alleyne resolved to try, if possible, to find another passage, and sent
Colonel Denison, with his crew of voyageurs, to examine another channel on the
north of the great island opposite us. I
rode on to Birti, and there found Colonel
Denison, who had succeeded in passing
through this northern channel, and reported
it, though difficult, by no means so bad as
the southern channel. Accordingly, on my
return, all troops not already committed to
the left bank were diverted into this channel; but seven companies of the Black
Watch had advanced too far to return with
safety. The troops worked till dusk, and
then bivouacked by half-battalions on the
high bank above their boats in the Rahami
cataract. The Cornwalls, with headquarters,
artillery, and convoy, bivouacked at Gamra.

On the following day (3d) the Cornwalls 3d Feb.
entered the cataract; and headquarters,

H

with the artillery and convoy, marched to
Birti, where, late in the evening, five companies of the Staffords arrived by the
northern passage after twelve hours' unre-
mitting toil. The whole of the remainder
of the infantry was still struggling through
the cataract; but the General had not hesi-
tated to push forward the convoy, there being
no fear of attack, and the ground at Birti
offering an admirable site for an encamp-
ment, and ample supplies of growing forage.

The Mudir's troops occupied the village
of Hush el Jeruf on the right bank opposite our camp, and Colvile reported that his
information was that the rebels had retired
beyond the Shukook pass, that no resistance was to be expected there, that Suleiman's movements were uncertain, and that
it was doubtful whether he had or had not
fled to Berber. One of our own spies,
however, brought us in apparently more
definite information. He said that Lekalik
and Moussa were encamped at the far end
of the Shukook pass; that they had given

Suleiman six days to collect his cattle and
family at Salamat, promising to hold the
pass for that time, but no longer; and that
then Suleiman was to go with Lekalik
across the desert to Abu Egli, Moussa
returning to his own country.

The mounted troops patrolled some six
miles to the front; and Colonel Butler reported that he had found a site for a camp
about this distance forward, which was
equally suitable for one battalion or for
two, with forage and good ground for
mounted troops, and that there was nothing
but clear water between it and Birti. The
General therefore decided to push forward
the mounted troops and the Staffords on
the following day.

Meanwhile the houses in Birti had been
carefully searched by our intelligence officers, and large quantities of papers found
were examined. Some few relics of Stewart's party were discovered, fragments of
French and English books, a portion of an
English "field boot," the broken face and

case of an aneroid barometer, which I have since ascertained was sold to Stewart an hour or two before his departure from Charing Cross with General Gordon. These were all found in Suleiman Wad Gamr's house. Every effort was made to ascertain correctly which houses, trees, and *sakyehs* were the property of Suleiman Wad Gamr, and of any prominent rebels; and a list of them was prepared.

For the first time since leaving Belal we found ourselves in a well-cultivated country. Birti was an oasis in the wilderness of hideous rocks, through which for ten days we had been wending our weary way. Both on the mainland and on the high hill island opposite there were many *sakyehs*, and plentiful green crops. Our commissariat officers, with the camels of the transport company, were engaged in searching for grain. Some was found in the houses, and much more buried in pits on the island.

The enemy's camp had been situated

on uncultivated ground, some distance below (down-stream of) the village of Birti
itself. A semicircle of low rocky hills surrounded it, the ends of the semicircle rest-
ing on the river. In the midst of it there
was a low rocky eminence; and on this,
on the slopes of the hills, and on the flat
ground below, the dervishes had constructed
their shelters of boughs of trees and straw
mats. One of the most curious features
of the camp was the number of places of
prayer of large size, prepared on spaces of
flat ground by clearing away all stones,
carefully marked out by lines of stones,
with the same point towards the east, with
which we are all familiar on oriental
prayer-carpets. Judging by my experience
of native camps built in a similar way in
Ashanti, I should say there had been from
1500 to 2000 men encamped here. We
could see where the tents of the three
chiefs had been, and the stables of their
horses. Nothing of any value was found
in the camp : a few cooking-pots, walking-

sticks, one or two pieces of wood with
verses from the Koran written on them,
some inferior straw mats, were all that we
could find. No arms of any kind were
discovered; but a thousand rounds of Remington ammunition were found in one of the
houses. The broad wady by which we had
purposed to march to the attack led directly
round the back of the camp to the cultivated ground behind, and had wide easy
passages leading right into the heart of the
camp. It was a matter of sore regret to
us not to have found the enemy here; and
it became evident to us that unless they
deliberately stayed to meet us, we never
could hope to overtake them. Already the
head of the Black Watch had been three
days in the Rahami cataract, and not a boat
had reached Birti.

4th Feb.   On the morning of the 4th, the Staffords
closed up at Birti, and six companies were
sent on by river, their advance covered by
the mounted troops. The leading companies arrived at the site selected by

Colonel Butler, and by him christened Castle Camp, at noon. Butler reconnoitred along the bank for between three and four miles farther over exceedingly broken ground, where horses had frequently to be led in single file. A mile and a half above Castle Camp the rapids began again; but Alleyne, who reconnoitred in his boat to their foot, and examined them, pronounced that they could be passed. A mile above Castle Camp, a large island (Dulka) began, and extended from three to four miles. On the opposite side of the island there appeared to be a stretch of clear water; but Alleyne, who examined it, discovered much broken water and many islands beyond.

During the day the Black Watch concentrated at Birti. They had been four days in the cataract, seven miles in length, working from dawn to dusk. They had lost one man drowned, and two boats. The last two companies of the Staffords were also kept at Birti, five of their boats

being in need of repair. They were all
ordered to advance to Castle Camp on the
5th; but no orders were issued for any advance beyond that place, pending Colonel
Butler's reconnaissance report, which did
not arrive till the following day.

A party of Royal Engineers and two companies of the Black Watch, under instructions of the intelligence officers, were employed in destroying Suleiman Wad Gamr's
houses, date-palms, and *sakyehs*.

The Cornwalls were still in Rahami cataract, and news arrived that the Gordons
had passed through Kab el Abd cataract.
A boat officer was sent back from Birti to
pilot them on, and to relieve the one who
had brought them through Edermih and
Kab el Abd.

General Earle hoped now to be able to
move the Cornwalls forward from Birti on
the 6th; and he therefore gave orders to
Colonel Colvile to instruct the Vakeel to
cross the Mudir's troops over on the 6th
to the left bank, with a view to their re-

maining in occupation of the Monassir country during our advance to Berber.

The General also, thinking that the Vakeel could be of great use to him in his advance as far as Salamat by collecting information, directed Colvile to request him to cross over with an escort on the 5th, in readiness to advance with our head-quarters on the 6th. Colvile was himself to come over, and to bring with him Suleiman's uncles and some other sheikhs who had surrendered to the Vakeel. This was in compliance with Lord Wolseley's orders that we were to take on to Berber all sheikhs who might come into our camp, as hostages for the good behaviour of their people in our rear.

Colvile heliographed back that the Vakeel did not wish to go any farther, saying his doing so would be contrary to the Mudir's orders, and that he was tired. He wished, however, to speak to General Earle, and would come across next day, bringing Abu Bekr and Wad el Turki.

He could not bring Omar, as he had run
away.

On the morning of the 5th General Earle
sent over to say, through Colvile, that he
was sorry the Vakeel found it inconvenient,
but must insist on his coming over and
accompanying the General to Salamat.   In
reply, the Vakeel wrote a letter saying his
advancing to Salamat would be useless, as
he did not know the country; that he had
orders from the Mudir to collect taxes at
Hamdab and in the cataracts by the help
of the Mudir's troops; that if he advanced
to Salamat, their collection would be delayed.   He could not disobey the Mudir's
orders; and he thought his remaining where
he was with the troops would have a good
effect, preventing the Monassir from returning.

General Earle still insisting upon his
point, the Vakeel at last gave way, con-
senting to bring his troops over, and to
accompany the General, but asserting it
would be impossible for him to start until

the 8th. General Earle then consented to give him an interview, and he came over to our camp. He protested with such apparent show of reason the utter uselessness of his going to Salamat, that General Earle consented to allow him to remain at Birti with the Mudir's troops, on condition that they crossed over on the morrow. To this the Vakeel consented promptly; and General Earle telegraphed to Lord Wolseley, asking him to urge the Mudir to insist on their remaining at Birti, at least till we should reach Abu Hamed.

With him the Vakeel had brought Abu Bekr, Suleiman Wad Gamr's uncle, and Wad el Turki; and they now remained in our camp. It was known that neither Abu Bekr nor Omar had been on friendly terms with Naaman, Suleiman's father, and they were not supposed to be on friendly terms with Suleiman himself; but a very compromising letter was found on Abu Bekr's person, written shortly after the murder by Suleiman, bidding Abu Bekr come to the

council to be held, and speaking of having
been occupied with the disposal of the
prisoners from the steamer. However,
Abu Bekr had come in under a promise of
safety; and as he was not actively a partic-
ipator in the murder, we were able to treat
him kindly, and use him as a guide.

Abd el Rahman Wad el Turki was a
sheikh of the Shagiyeh tribe. He had
fought against the Mudir's troops at Deb-
beh and at Korti, having raised a small
force. After the defeat at Korti, he had
retired to the rocks above Edermih cataract, and had collected another force there.
He had remained there till our advance,
when he retired to Birti, and joined the
Robatab under Moussa, bringing with him
a contingent of about 100 men. He was a
great partisan of the Mahdi.

Colonel Butler's reconnaissance reports
having arrived during the night of the 4th.
General Earle informed him, on the morning of the 5th, that he did not wish any
advance in boats beyond Castle Camp

until the two channels in front had been more thoroughly examined. " Lieut.-Colonel Alleyne," the instructions run, "should push boat-reconnaissance up both channels until he has discovered which is the best, and should examine the ground with a view to sites for camping, while you are making an extended reconnaissance towards the front." The Black Watch and remainder of the Staffords were sent on to Castle Camp, and Colonel Butler was told to order the advance of the Staffords on the following day to such point as he might consider best after reconnaissance and consultation with Alleyne. Butler was requested to make his reconnaissance early, so that his report might arrive before sundown, as no further orders would be issued till it arrived. With General Earle's memorandum, a boy, who had been captured in the Mahdi's uniform, and who said that he had deserted from the rebel camp at Shukook, was sent to act as a guide.

While the Staffords and Black Watch

were advancing to Castle Camp, the Cornwalls were arriving at Birti; and as they
arrived, they were employed completing the
destruction of the houses, palm-trees, and
sakyehs of Suleiman Wad Gamr, his uncle
Omar, and other prominent rebels. Nothing is easier than to destroy a *sakyeh*, its
timber and rope burning freely. We
found that by an occasional charge of gun-
cotton, and by the free use of pickaxes, we
could rapidly level the largest mud-built
house to the ground. But the destruction
of palm-trees is a difficult matter. The
tough fibrous bark blunts the axes, and the
tree will not burn freely; nevertheless some
280 date-palms were cut down or utterly
destroyed by fire.

The Commissariat continued their search
for grain; and it was reported to me that
our horses were now rationed with grain
up to the 6th March, and our natives with
flour to 23d March, without counting six tons
of unground wheat to be used for either
natives or horses as most required. From

Hamdab to Birti no supplies of any kind, except growing forage, had been obtainable either by capture or purchase. The country had been a desolate waste; the people had buried their grain in the desert, and driven off their cattle. By no offers could they be induced to bring even milk for sale, and by no promise of wage could they be tempted to engage in our service as labourers.

That afternoon, about four o'clock, a cipher-telegram arrived from General Wood, who, we thus learned, was acting as Chief of the Staff in place of Sir R. Buller. General Earle and I deciphered it together. It ran thus: "4th Feb., 8.50 P.M.—I am ordered by Lord Wolseley to inform you that, to his deep regret, Khartoum was found by Wilson to be in possession of enemy. Wilson in returning was wrecked, but steamer has gone for him, and there is no apparent danger for him. You are to halt where you are until further orders."

It is needless to say what we felt. Any

thought for ourselves was swallowed up in grief for what we could only interpret to mean Gordon's certain death. Both of us felt, too, how great the shock would be to Lord Wolseley; and to me there was a peculiar sting in the fact of this blow coming upon the anniversary of the capture of Coomassie. But action had to be at once taken, and immediate orders were sent to Colonel Butler that none of his troops were to move without further orders,—that he was to patrol with small bodies of cavalry only, and hold all his troops ready to move at short notice. Colvile was instructed that the Mudir's troops were not to cross on the morrow; and, convinced in his own mind, as I was in mine, that we should be at once recalled, General Earle would not bring the Gordon Highlanders to Birti, but sent back his aide-de-camp with orders to them to close up at Gamra, construct a zareeba, and halt there till further orders. The officer sent with the order failed to find them, as they had not reached Gamra, where he fully expected they would be; and darkness came on before he could go farther. The order, however, reached them on the following morning early. The contents of the telegram were kept strictly secret, no one but General Earle and myself knowing the cause of the orders to halt.

The evening brought us the report of Colonel Butler's reconnaissance. It has a singular interest by the light of subsequent events. He had proceeded in the direction of the Shukook pass, getting out to the river whenever practicable. He had ascended a high range of hills near the upper end of the large island (Dulka) about six to seven miles distant from his camp—a range which he described as continued across the several branches of the river, its highest point being attained in a large dome-shaped hill on the island of Boni, which overlaps Dulka. For more than an hour previously, the native boy we had sent him had constantly been informing him that Shukook was only a very short distance ahead—on several occasions point-

ing out what he called the entrance to the
pass, amid the rugged surrounding rocks.
Now, however, from the top of the hill he
pointed out a place two miles distant as the
real Shukook, and asserted that a lower
range lying between him and it was immediately over the enemy's camp. Colonel
Butler had found one or two sites which
would do for a camp. The ridge which he
had ascended was that on which, five days
later, we fought the action of Kirbekan.

Alleyne had proceeded up the southern
channel to the foot of the rapids, and then
walked on the shore of the island nearly
two miles farther. He pronounced the
channel practicable. The northern channel
was a maze of islands, rocks, and rapid
water.

In acknowledging his instructions not to
move till further orders, Butler reported
later that his camel-corps patrol had fallen
in with the enemy, exchanged shots, brought
in a prisoner, and captured some camels,
goats, and cattle. We afterwards found

they had come across a party of armed villagers tending their flocks in a desert wady.

Before the arrival of the telegram telling us of the fall of Khartoum, a long telegram had been sent to Lord Wolseley detailing the position of the troops and the latest news of the enemy. General Earle said in this that he did not anticipate resistance this side of Abu Hamed, and would push on as rapidly as possible, consistently with the necessary precautions. "The road beyond this," he said, "is as bad as the river —a tangled mass of rocks, quite unsuited for mounted troops, and affording neither good anchorage nor good ground for bivouacs." We had informed Colonel Rundle at Korosko of our advance beyond Birti having commenced; and in addition to our previous urgent demands for boat-repairing materials and paint, horse-shoes and nails, to be sent to meet us at Abu Hamed, we now added a moving appeal for trousers, telegraphing: "Men's and many officers' trousers in rags; not sufficient for decency."

Lord Wolseley was now informed that his telegram had been received, and that his instructions were being carried out; and Rundle was advised that the probable date of our arrival at Salamat, which we had given as the 10th February, must now be postponed.

6th Feb. Early on the 6th I rode over to Colonel Butler's camp, and, by General Earle's permission, told him, under the seal of secrecy, the contents of yesterday's telegram. General Earle rode back to Gamra and visited the Gordon Highlanders.

All the troops had a day of thorough rest, much needed after the unending labours of the past fortnight. It gave them the opportunity of washing their clothes and trying to patch the particoloured rags they were wearing as trousers. General Earle talked over with me the arrangements to be made for the return to Korti, which we confidently expected would be ordered; and we sent a party of the Egyptian camel corps back to Abu Dom to act as carriers of messages, requesting the commandants there to send us all messages from Lord Wolseley in duplicate — one copy by two of our own camel-men, one copy by a native messenger. And as our stay at Birti might possibly be prolonged, we made sanitary arrangements for supply of water, &c., as for a standing camp.

In the evening Colvile reported that a man had just come in with the news that the enemy, who were in Shukook, had advanced to Kirbekan; that they were not a thousand strong, and had about 150 rifles. They had no outposts at night, but sent out a patrol before daylight. He said they had chosen their present camp as being easier to escape from than Shukook in case of defeat. This information was at once sent to Colonel Butler.

On the 7th the troops were employed in im- 7th Feb. proving the sanitary condition and watering arrangements of the camps. A quantity of grain was discovered by our foraging-parties on Ishishi island, and was brought over to our camp. We had now not only full loads

of grain for all our camels, but were able
out of the surplus to issue a small grain-
ration to the camels which had hitherto
been subsisting on growing crops only.
Our camels were in fair condition, but from
want of sufficient work were becoming soft,
and the saddle-galls from which these un-
fortunate animals seem seldom or never
free were in consequence not so healthy.
We found it necessary to exercise the camels
regularly, which had a better effect on their
health than even the issue of grain.   Butler
sent out patrols to the scene of the camel
corps skirmish of the 5th, without finding
any trace of the enemy.

8th Feb.   On the morning of the 8th we sent to the
Chief of the Staff a telegram stating the
exact state of our supplies, based upon re-
turns obtained during the halt.   We told
him that the total strength drawing rations
last night was 2966 officers and men, and
fixed the exact number of days' supply of
each article remaining for that number; and
we requested him so to arrange that the

supplies sent by Rundle to Korosko should equalise the various articles of food. We added that we had thirty days' grain for our 140 horses, but none for our 580 camels; that the latter had hitherto done well on the green forage of the country, but that a prolonged halt would make it very difficult to feed them. Soap we especially asked for to be sent up by first convoy. We had only thirty days' supply remaining; and many of the boats were full of lice, which were infesting the clothes of the men, and in some cases of the officers.

CHAPTER VIII.

KIRBEKAN—RECONNAISSANCE AND PREPARATION.

8th Feb.

AT 8 A.M. on Sunday the 8th, General Earle received a message from General Wood, dated 1 A.M., 7th: "Lord Wolseley," it said, " is communicating with Government as to future operations, but he wishes you to push on to Abu Hamed, and await further orders there."

Orders were at once issued and despatched for the Gordons to advance immediately by the northern channel to Birti, and for the Staffords, covered by the mounted troops, to advance from Castle Camp to a point to be selected by Colonel Butler. General Earle did not wish to commit more than one battalion to the rapids, until their nature was more thoroughly known, and therefore he left the Black Watch at Castle Camp. Wishing to close up the Gordons nearer to the Cornwalls, he left the latter also for the day at Birti. The Black Watch and a wing of the Cornwalls were ordered to advance on the 9th, and the Mudir's troops to cross over to the left bank.

I rode over with the orders to Castle Camp, and found the men in their red coats, after church parade. Within half an hour Alleyne and the first boats were off, and the cavalry scouts were advancing along the bank.

Butler, taking command of the whole advanced guard, left the Staffords at the head of the first rapid, and directed Colonel Eyre to make his camp on Dulka island. He then advanced with Major Flood and twenty Hussars along the left bank. At 2.30 P.M. his scouts fell in with the enemy, posted on some rocky ground, all of which had been patrolled by our mounted troops on the 5th.

Their right rested on the river, and they
were dotted about clumps of rock commanding the track by which the cavalry
were advancing. Our men took up a position opposite them and fired a few volleys,
which made them leave the front faces of
the rocky knolls, but they still held their
sides and summits. About 4 P.M. four ex-
ploring boats arrived by river just below the
cavalry, and Butler landed two boats' crews
and fired some volleys. Colonel Butler estimated those who had shown themselves as
about 200 in number. Only about ten rifles
had opened fire, but he had seen many
spear-heads. At the approach of sunset
Butler retired to Castle Camp, the enemy
following him as far as the most advanced
position which he had held. The boats fell
back to Colonel Eyre's camp on Dulka
island.

Colonel Butler reported the position occupied by the enemy as being about two miles
from Colonel Eyre's camp on Dulka island,
with the river between; and he considered

that the Staffords could be moved to the spot where he engaged the enemy in less than two hours, and the Black Watch from Castle Camp in six hours. Colonel Butler said that he would cover the ground for the Staffords landing next day with his mounted troops, and then move the battalion to the left bank, bringing the Black Watch also to the same place, unless otherwise ordered. He asked for two guns to be sent early next day to Castle Camp; and in his report stated that the enemy's right and rear was within easy range of Dulka island, so that guns taken across the river by boat, and carried about two miles along the island, could take the position in reverse. He sent his staff officer, Lieutenant Pirie, with the report.

On receipt of this report at 10 P.M., and after questioning Lieutenant Pirie, General Earle decided that he would himself reconnoitre the position on the following day. He ordered the two guns asked for to Castle Camp, but did not wish them sent over to

Dulka island. He told Colonel Butler that
he would leave Birti at 6.30 A.M. for Castle
Camp, and directed that an officer should
be left there to guide him to the position
where he would find Colonel Butler. He
approved of the proposal to move the Staffords and Black Watch to the open ground
in rear of the position opposite the enemy
occupied by the cavalry; and impressed the
importance of great care in effecting the
crossing of the Staffords, so that it should
be impossible for them to be attacked while
landing, in case the enemy should advance
and compel our cavalry to retire.

9th Feb.   On the morning of the 9th, the following
instructions were sent to Colonel Colvile:
the Mudir's troops, after crossing the river,
were to take up a position out of rifle-range
of our Birti camp. Headquarters were about
to advance, but half a battalion of the Cornwalls would remain at Birti, where the Gordons were expected to arrive that day.
Should they do so, all our troops would
clear out of Birti on the morning of the

10th, and Colonel Colvile should himself
then join General Earle's headquarters.
Before leaving, Colvile was to inform the
Vakeel that he and the Mudir's troops were
to remain in occupation of the Monassir
country till further orders,—General Earle
relying upon the Vakeel to obtain and forward to us supplies of cattle and grain, to
send us information of the movements and
intentions of the enemy, and to forward our
messages to and from Abu Dom.

By 11 A.M. the Mudir's troops had crossed
and bivouacked opposite their former camp.
Shortly after landing, they found the moun-
tain-gun from Colonel Stewart's steamer.
It was spiked, and the sight, spokes of one
wheel, and cap-squares were missing.

General Earle's start from Birti was
somewhat delayed; and when we moved on
from Castle Camp, the officer sent to guide
us unfortunately could not find the way, and
lost himself amongst the rocks, so that we
did not reach the ground where the Staffords
were to encamp until nearly mid-day.

Meanwhile the mounted troops had pushed forward, and had occupied with their advanced posts the rocky hillocks, or koppies, as they are called in South Africa, which they had occupied yesterday, and found the enemy still in the same position as before.   Colonel Butler then sent for the Staffords.

General Earle, accompanied by his staff, then personally examined the enemy's position from the rocks upon which our cavalry vedettes were posted, about 800 yards distant.   Immediately in front of us the enemy held some rocky koppies about 50 to 80 feet in height, their right being directly over the river.   Between two of these koppies ran the road from Birti to Salamat. We could see that they had built stone sconces, or breastworks, among the rocks, and completely commanded with their rifles both road and river.   They must clearly be turned out of that before we could advance to Abu Hamed.

Running parallel to the low rocky koppies

above-named, but to the enemy's left rear, and some 600 yards behind the koppies, and ending abruptly 600 yards from the river, was a very remarkable ridge about 300 feet high, presenting on the side next to us a steep slope like the moraine of a glacier, out of which at the summit projected a ridge of white marble rocks, as the teeth project from the jawbone of a skeleton. This was the ridge ascended by Colonel Butler on the 5th. All along its summit we could see men with flags and spear-heads moving about among the rocks. Still it was evident that these two positions were not capable of holding a large body of men; and we were disposed to believe them held by an outpost some 300 to 400 strong, and that we should find the enemy emerge in force from behind the hills on our advancing to attack them.

There were four ways of attacking the position. First, the direct attack upon the koppies, aided perhaps by flanking fire from Dulka island. This would involve heavy loss, and would be the least effectual, as the enemy, when beaten, would retreat directly along the river, through the broken ground, to the Shukook pass. Secondly, an advance through the valley, between the range of koppies and the marble-topped high ridge. This would turn the koppies; and General Earle inclined to the belief, in which I shared, that if once the enemy in the koppies found themselves outflanked, and liable to have their retreat cut off, they would retreat. Thirdly, to advance upon the marble-topped ridge, and storm it, bringing fire from it to bear afterwards upon the koppies below, while we sent a force to attack them. Fourthly, provided the country would lend itself to the idea, to move to our right under cover of the broken ground, and march completely round the marble-topped ridge, which was only about a mile long, and move round its rear to the attack both of it and of the koppies. Colonel Butler was sent at 4 P.M. to make a wide detour round the ridge, and see if there was a fair road for infantry and camels by which we could thus turn the position. On his return he reported that we could turn the position by an easy march through a wide sandy wady, and that he had noted a road by which we could approach the wady from our camp without exposing ourselves to any great extent. This latter plan of advance was therefore decided upon by the General; and as the enemy did not appear to be in great force, it was resolved to attack him the following morning, with such troops as we had ready to our hand.

Sending over to Castle Camp for the two guns to come on, and also for the senior medical officer, with such assistance as he might require, and having informed him of what was in contemplation, we then proceeded to organise the details for the morrow's fight.

By sunset the whole of the Staffords, with two sections of the field-hospital, and the headquarters and seven companies of the

K

Black Watch, had reached their bivouac, a short mile from the enemy's position. One company of the Black Watch was absent. Having taken the wrong channel, and been fired upon from the right bank, it had returned to Castle Camp, and bivouacked there with the wing of the Cornwalls, who arrived there from Birti. The two guns arrived, and the senior medical officer, with his staff and certain necessary appliances; and the following dispositions for the attack were made.

One company of the Black Watch, under Lieut.-Colonel Eden, with Major Sandwith as his staff officer, was to remain in the zareeba, to guard the boats and baggage. All infantry baggage to be packed in the boats by 6.30 A.M.; all other baggage and baggage-animals to be parked on the low shore, in front of the boats. All headquarter servants, departmental and unarmed men, to remain with the baggage. The boat of the Royal Navy, with its Gatling gun so disposed as to sweep the shore and river up-stream, to be under Lieut.-Colonel Eden's command.

The Staffords and six companies Black Watch, with the two guns, to parade in sufficient time to march off the ground at seven o'clock. Troops in red, Highlanders in kilts. The men to breakfast before parade, and carry one day's rations of meat and biscuit. All water-bottles to be full on marching off. Each man to carry sixty rounds of ammunition, and each battalion to have two camels, each carrying four boxes of reserve ammunition, making 4800 rounds of reserve ammunition for each battalion. The guns to have two ammunition-camels for each gun. Commanding officers, two wing field-officers, and the adjutant of each battalion, to be mounted.

Each battalion to have eight stretchers carried by sixteen of its unarmed men, with four men in reserve as bearers. A detachment of the field-hospital, with three camels carrying surgical and hospital equipment, to parade with the infantry; also two camels to carry water for the field-hospital.

The Hussars and camel corps to parade separately under Colonel Butler.

General Brackenbury, Major Boyle, Major Slade, Captain Beaumont, and Lieutenant St Aubyn to accompany General Earle. All other staff officers to remain with the baggage, except Lieut.-Colonel Alleyne, who was instructed to take command of two companies of the Staffords and the two guns, and to occupy with them the rocky position held yesterday by our cavalry outposts, and to hold the enemy in check in front, attracting their attention in that direction while our flank movement was in progress.

During the afternoon the enemy opened fire from a small island above Dulka island, and one of their shots having struck one of our vedettes, a company of the Staffords was sent across in boats to occupy the island and bivouack there. To reach the island, the boats had to ascend a nasty

rapid just opposite our bivouac.   All fires
were put out at "lights out," and it was
ordered that none should be lit before *réveillé* on the following day.

About 3 P.M. a telegram arrived from
Lord Wolseley to the following effect—
dated 9 A.M., 8th : The Government have
decided that the Mahdi's power at Khartoum must be overthrown.   This most
probably means a campaign here next cold
weather, and certainly the retention in the
Soudan of all troops now here.   A strong
force of all arms goes as soon as possible to
Suakim to crush Osman Digma.   We must
now take Berber.   Buller will now take
Metemmeh.   Let me know early the date
you calculate upon reaching Berber, so that
Buller's force may co-operate with you.

At 5.45 P.M. a long letter arrived from
Lord Wolseley to General Earle, dated 2
P.M., 7th.   It was almost entirely in cipher,
and I sat up till late in the night decipher-
ing its contents.   In it Lord Wolseley in-

formed General Earle of the questions he
had addressed to the Cabinet, the replies
he had received, and his further queries.
It amplified the contents of his telegram
received that afternoon.   It told us that he
had not yet heard of Wilson's safety; and
in it there was this sentence : " I congratulate you upon the progress you have made,
although I am naturally very sorry the
enemy have not tested the temper of your
steel.   However, let us hope their courage
may be stiffened by the fall of Khartoum,
and that you may strike them hard yet
before you reach Berber."   Hope soon to
be realised!

General Earle talked this letter over with
me until a very late hour, and decided not
to reply to it till after the action of the
morrow.   Two of our spies came in, and
professed to have been unable to see any
trace of the enemy in the position they had
held during the day; and we retired to rest,
half fearing they might again give us the

slip, as they had done ten days before at Birti. But we were needlessly anxious. We did not then know that their courage had been stiffened — that they had heard of the fall of Khartoum.

CHAPTER IX.

KIRBEKAN—THE FIGHT.

THE night passed without incident. At the earliest dawn our cavalry vedettes were again in their position of yesterday, and as soon as the growing daylight enabled them to see clearly, they reported the enemy still in position—good news which soon spread through the camp. The men were tired of the delays caused by the precautions necessary in the presence of an enemy who escaped just as we were within striking distance; and those holding responsible positions in the force felt it to be of the utmost importance to meet the enemy soon, and get the chance of teaching them a lesson which would prevent their meeting

10th Feb.

us again for some time, thus clearing the
way for our advance to the main objective
of our column—Berber.

The company on outpost-duty at Dulka
island was recalled, baggage was parked
according to orders, the naval boat was
placed in position, the camels were loaded
to accompany the column. The men
breakfasted and fell in on parade, looking
smart and thoroughly workmanlike. After
inspection, Lieut.-Colonel Eden's company
of the Black Watch was set to work forming a small zareeba; two companies of the
Staffordshire Regiment were told off to
escort the two guns under Lieut.-Colonel
Alleyne; and as soon as we saw the dispositions for defence of the zareeba fairly
complete, and Alleyne's two companies and
guns marched off to occupy the ground held
by our cavalry outposts, with orders not to
open fire till we had reached the outer
flank of the great ridge round which we
were to move, the column marched off. It
was then about a quarter past seven. Just

before we left the zareeba, General Earle
directed me to send back to inform the
English correspondent of a foreign news-
paper, who had made his way up with the
Gordon Highlanders, that, owing to the
necessity for economising all food for man
and beast, and in view of all spare whaler
accommodation being required for transport
of sick, he could not allow any civilian
correspondents to accompany the column.

We marched in line of half-battalion
columns, at an interval of two companies,
the Staffords (six companies) leading, the
Black Watch (six companies) following.
Company stretcher-bearers followed their
own companies. The field-hospital camels
and reserve small-arm ammunition camels
(nine and one spare), were massed between
the Staffords and Black Watch, and moved
with the left column. The General's object
in this formation was to enable each column
to take advantage of practicable ground for
marching as long as we were moving over
the rocks, but at the same time to be able,

by closing the columns together, to get rapidly into formation ready to form square, or rather oblong, with the stretcher-bearers and camels inside.

Colonel Butler led the column. The first mile of our road lay in a north-easterly direction over broken but hard ground; then we reached a wide wady of loose deep sand, in which progress was slow and fatiguing, and followed it till we reached the farthest end of the marble-topped ridge. We then, at about half-past eight, halted for a few minutes, allowing a few men to fall out. Not a shot had been fired at us as yet, though our column must have been visible from the ridge at more than one point in its march. While here we heard Alleyne's guns open fire.

Our front as we marched had been covered by the cavalry; our left flank by the Egyptian camel corps, who lined the edge of the broken ground opposite to the high ridge. Colonel Butler now went on with the cavalry scouts, and just as we were

about to continue our march, sent back to
say that the enemy were in sight on some
low rocky hills, to the number of two or
three hundred, and immediately afterwards
a second message to say the enemy were
retiring. We now marched round the
eastern end of the ridge, and turning sharp
to the left, marched through a rocky valley
in the direction of the river, with the high
ridge on our left. In front of us was a low
rocky range running at right angles to the
high ridge on which Colonel Butler had
seen the enemy. The enemy now opened
fire on us from the high ridge at about
9.15 A.M., and we had two or three men hit.
General Earle, after a short farther advance,
halted the column under cover, and sent
forward one company of the Staffords to
the low range in front, and another company (C) to line the rocks on our left, and
keep down the fire from the high ridge.
The enemy not appearing immediately in
front, the column advanced about 300
yards into a valley with rocky ridges on

every side, leaving C Company of the Staffords engaged with the enemy on the high ridge. The fire from this ridge now becoming hotter, General Earle directed Colonel Eyre to take two companies of his regiment and endeavour to take the ridge by its western shoulder. They advanced under a heavy fire, and climbed about one third of the way up the shoulder, till they reached a cluster of rocks under which they obtained partial shelter.

At the same time two companies of the Black Watch descended the rocky ridge to our right front, from whence the river was visible about six hundred yards away; and we could see parties of the enemy making their way to it, and swimming over to the opposite bank. It being then evident that the only serious opposition we had to expect was from the enemy remaining on the high marble-topped ridge, and on the koppies, whence fire was now opened on us, General Earle ordered two companies of the Black Watch to move to their right front towards

the river-bank, and establish themselves
there, so as to prevent all retreat in this
direction; and the three remaining companies of the Staffords and the four remaining companies of the Black Watch to
advance and swing round to the left, so as
to face the koppies.

It now became evident, from the fire
which was directed upon us from the
koppies, that the enemy had a considerable
body of riflemen in position there, and the
two companies of the Black Watch which
had been sent down to the river were
ordered to advance in line along the river-
bank towards the koppies, clearing it of the
enemy.

The remainder of the Black Watch and
Staffords took up a position on the rocks, at
about 800 yards, and brought a heavy fire
to bear upon the koppies. Little by little
they advanced from one vantage-point to
another, till they attained a position on the
nearest rocks to the koppies, about 400
yards distant. Between them and the

koppies there was now only open ground,
swept by the enemy's fire.

General Earle now ordered the two
companies of the Black Watch nearest the
river, who had by this time come up abreast
of our main position, to advance along the
shore of the low Nile, under cover of the
high bank, and take the koppie nearest the
river from its river flank. A company
of the Staffords accompanied them, and
advancing rapidly under cover of the river-
bank, they seized the lowest rocks and then
the summit of this koppie, driving out or
killing the rebels who were there. Some
of these attempted flight by the river in the
direction of Colonel Alleyne's men and our
zareeba; a few escaped by swimming, but
many were shot down by our men. From
the summit of this koppie now in our hands,
a flanking fire was brought to bear upon the
two main central koppies.

It was now evident that nothing more
was to be done but to assault the position,
and the order was about to be given when

a body of the enemy, one of whom carried
a flag, the rest being armed with spears,
descended boldly from the heights in front,
and charged towards the nearest companies
of the Black Watch, which were somewhat
advanced towards our left front, under
Colonel Green. The troops never moved,
but the gallant Arabs were received with
so withering a fire from all sides that those
who were not killed turned and fled towards
the river. A few gained it. Our men, far
from fearing the rush, stood up to meet it,
in some cases even advanced; and they
could with difficulty be restrained from
leaving the ranks to follow the fugitives
along the river.

This episode over, the order for the
assault was given, and well responded to.
I had myself previously carried the orders
to the troops on the koppie by the river
to advance simultaneously with the front
assault, and had returned to General Earle
to the front of the position previous to the
enemy's charge. General Earle ordered

the assault to be made; and then, with pipes
playing, the Black Watch charged over the
open ground and stormed the koppies, not
stopping till they had crowned the highest
rocks. The troops on the river-side koppie
also well carried out their orders, advancing from the flank and seizing the koppie
nearest to them. Such of the enemy as
still remained fought to the last, and were
killed to a man.

The assault was over, and the two main
koppies were in our hands; the troops were
searching the sconces and holes among the
rocks; and there was, as there must always
be after such an effort, some need to collect
them and form them up for fresh work.
Between the crests of the two main koppies
there was a depression forming a small flat
plateau, on which was built a stone hut
some ten feet square, with a thatched roof.
General Earle was engaged in forming up
the men in the ranks on this plateau, not
more than ten yards from the hut, when a
sergeant of the Black Watch said, "There

L

are a lot of men in that hut, and they have just shot one of our men." General Earle ordered the roof to be set on fire; but on its being said that there was a quantity of ammunition in the hut, he ordered the roof to be pulled down, and himself approached the hut. I was close to him, and said, "Take care, sir; the hut is full of men." Our men had set the roof on fire, and my attention was attracted for a moment by seeing a native who rushed out from the side door of the hut bayoneted by one of our men. As I turned my head back towards the General, I saw him fall, shot through the head from a small square window in the hut, close to which he had approached. He lived only a few minutes, tended to the last by his aide-de-camp Lieutenant St Aubyn, and by the senior medical officer, Surgeon-Major Harvey.

The command having now devolved upon me, I directed two companies of the Black Watch to remain as a picket on the koppies; and I had sent to the Staffords

with a view to assembling them, when it
was brought to my knowledge that the two
companies of the Staffords sent to take the
high ridge had failed as yet to reach higher
than the cluster of rocks about one-third of
the way up; that Colonel Eyre had been
killed, shot through the heart; that Captain
Horsburgh and Lieutenant Colborne had
been severely wounded; that their loss in
men had been considerable; that their ammunition was exhausted, except four rounds
per man, which they had reserved; and that
the enemy was still holding the ridge. Assembling, therefore, four companies of the
Black Watch as a reserve at the foot of the
koppies, I sent for Lieutenant-Colonel Beale,
upon whom the command of the Staffords
had devolved, and instructed him to take
the remainder of his regiment, reinforce the
two companies on the hill with troops and
ammunition, and with the aid of the company left to watch the hill early in the day,
assault and take the position. The order
was most admirably carried out. Ascend-

ing the steep moraine-like hill by alternate
rushes, the Staffords reached the rocky
summit, and bayoneted the enemy, who
remained there fighting to the very end.

It was now about one o'clock, and the
enemy were driven from their last position.
Meanwhile, early in the day, Colonel Butler, with the few Hussars at his disposal, had
struck the river above the point where we
first gained it, and had pursued scattered
groups of Arabs who were retreating along
the main river track. Half an hour later
he gained the entrance to the Shukook
pass, and in the centre of the rocky gorge
there came upon the enemy's deserted
camp, where he captured a number of
standards, and some camels and donkeys.
While there the enemy opened fire upon
the Hussars from the surrounding hills, but
without causing any casualties among our
men. Colonel Butler sent back for camel-
men to drive in the animals captured : the
message did not reach me till after the
fight, and the camel corps having then been

fighting for the whole morning, I instructed Colonel Butler to return with the cavalry to camp. He had already anticipated this order, driving back some of the animals with the Hussars.

The Egyptian camel corps under Major Marriott had done excellent service. They had at the commencement of the day taken up a position in front of the high ridge, and protected the flank of the infantry in its advance. In that position they remained throughout the day, assisting by their fire to keep down the fire from the heights, and shooting, or in some instances pursuing and capturing, the rebels who attempted to escape towards the east, along the southern slope of the hill. Their conduct was witnessed by the Staffords, who remained so long upon the shoulder of the hill, and was the theme of much praise. When the Staffords stormed the hill one Egyptian soldier charged up the hill, all alone, on their extreme right—a most gallant feat. They had two men killed and one wounded.

Leaving, as already said, two companies of the Black Watch on the summit of the koppies, and sending two companies to bivouac on a high Nile island at the head of the rapid, about a mile and a half up the river, I ordered the remainder of the troops back to camp.

During the action the wounded had been collected, as far as possible, by the stretcher-bearers into groups under shelter from fire; dressing-stations had been established at successive points as we moved on; and restoratives, such as beef-tea prepared on the field, champagne, and brandy, were administered to the wounded during and after the action. Owing to the nature of the ground, both medical officers and wounded had been frequently exposed to considerable cross-fire. The medical officers of corps had accompanied their men into action, and. the medical officers of the dressing-station gave their services freely wherever most required. As soon as the action was over, additional men were told off as stretcher-bearers, and the wounded were brought into our camp. The bodies of General Earle, Colonel Eyre, and Colonel Coveney, were conveyed back to our camp; the other brave dead were buried together by the river-bank, near the field where they had fallen.

At sunset the bodies of General Earle, Colonel Eyre, and Colonel Coveney were buried side by side in deep graves near the foot of a solitary palm-tree; and the hill of Kirbekan echoed back the boom of the minute-guns paying their solemn tribute to the memory of three soldiers, each a type of what the English officer should be.

Orders were then issued for the half-battalion of the Cornwalls, which had arrived in camp during the day, together with the two companies of the Staffords and the two companies of the Black Watch which had not been engaged in the flank march, to advance by river in the morning, and occupy the position at the head of the rapid, relieving the two companies of the

Black Watch there, and for the remainder
of the Cornwalls who had reached Castle
Camp to come on to our camp. I wished
now to put the Cornwalls and Gordons in
front; but the latter, to my disappointment,
had not got farther than Birti, their progress
through the northern channel of the Rahami cataract having been, owing to the
falling Nile, slower than that of the other
troops who had traversed the same passage.
They were ordered to come on as soon as
possible.

It was a busy night. There was much to
be thought of and arranged. I sent off a
telegraphic summary and a written despatch,
and a letter to Lord Wolseley, in which I
said, "Our troops having turned them out
of these positions, must have a great effect
upon the spirit of the enemy. I sincerely
trust it may prevent our having to fight
our way to Abu Hamed, as if we have
many such fights as to-day, we shall be
seriously embarrassed how to carry on our

wounded. If it enables us to pass the Shukook pass, which is still before us, and to get through the rapids ahead without more fighting, it will indeed be a valuable day for us."

We had not purchased our victory cheaply. General Earle, Colonel Eyre, Colonel Coveney, and nine men killed; four officers and forty-four men wounded, made a total of sixty,—a serious loss in our little force of twelve hundred. It had been most difficult to estimate either the enemy's strength or his loss with accuracy. I do not believe that when we marched to attack the position there were more than about eight hundred men holding it. Half of these made their escape before we attacked; a few more during the fight. The remainder were simply desperate men, resolved to fight to the last, and to sell their lives dearly. They were in what might fairly have been called an impregnable position, and they were thoroughly well armed,—a position out of which they could

not have been dislodged by any but first-
rate troops. We have all heard of "a position which ten men could hold against a
thousand." I honestly confess that the
expression conveys exactly what was in my
mind when first I saw the hills we had to
attack.

In my despatch written that night, I gave
the probable loss of the enemy as not less
than a hundred and fifty. This I altered
to two hundred after going over the ground
next day with Colonel Butler. We counted
sixty dead bodies on the main koppies,
sixty-five on the razor-backed ridge ; others
were lying below ; there were many whom
we could not have seen ; many had been
shot crossing the river : and I am satisfied
now that the larger figure does not over-
state the enemy's loss.

Not less valuable than the effect of this
action upon the enemy's *morale* was its
effect upon the spirits of our own men. It
inspired them with great confidence. The

idea that unless in square formation they could not stand against Arabs had been to a certain extent prevalent : to-day the troops had learnt that they could beat their enemy in hand-to-hand combats in the rocks, fighting in loose order.

CHAPTER X.

THE SHUKOOK PASS.

11th Feb. ON the morning of the 11th, the troops began to pass through the troublesome rapid commencing opposite our camp, and a wing of the Cornwalls, two companies of the Black Watch, and two of the Staffords — all troops which had not been engaged on the previous day — reached the high Nile island at Kirbekan, and camped there, relieving the companies of the Black Watch who had bivouacked there the preceding night. The mounted troops covered the advance, and Butler reconnoitred to the entrance of, and some distance into, the Shukook pass, seeing no sign of any enemy. The other wing of the Cornwalls, the artillery and convoy, arrived in our camp opposite Dulka island, and the Gordons reached Castle Camp.

Now was the time when a strong force of cavalry would have been invaluable. To push on after the enemy with cavalry, and at once seize and hold the upper end of the Shukook pass, before he could rally from his defeat, was the proper course to pursue. It could not be done with infantry, for the infantry were tied to their boats, and every man who marched a yard beyond his boat, had to be marched back again to it sooner or later. As for mounted troops, all that could be spared, after leaving the strictly necessary guards with the main camp, the artillery and convoy, were about sixty Hussars, and forty to fifty of the Egyptian camel corps; and to push on so small a force to encamp at the far side of this long and difficult pass without any infantry support, would have been to court disaster. The mounted troops, therefore, fell back to the bivouac at Kirbekan.

Slade examined nine prisoners whom we
had taken in the action of yesterday, and
reported that, from their statements, the
enemy who had held the position consisted
of 400 men of the Robatab tribe, under
Sheikh Moussa Wad Abu Hegel; 200 men
from Berber, under Sheikh Ali Wad Hus-
sein and Hamid Lekalik, cousin and brother
respectively of Abdul Majid Wad el Lekalik; 300 of the Monassir tribe, under Sheikh
el Hagid; and several slaves and villagers
from their lands,—making a total of about
1500 to 2000 men, of whom the Robatab
and Berber men alone had held the position
so stoutly defended. All the sheikhs above-
named, with the exception of El Hagid,
were killed during the action, Moussa's
body having been identified by one of the
prisoners. The main camp of the enemy
was at the upper end of the Shukook pass,
the camp taken by our mounted troops at
the lower end of the pass being only an
advanced post. The prisoners stated that
neither Suleiman Wad Gamr nor Abdul

Majid Wad el Lekalik had been present at
the action, the former being at Salamat, the
latter at the main camp.   They said that
their losses had been very heavy, only
those who escaped by swimming the river
having been saved.   They all agreed in
stating that after the enemy left Birti, they
had retired to the spot where the main
camp now was, at the upper end of the
Shukook pass, and that they had returned
and occupied the position at Kirbekan on
the 6th, strengthening the position by reinforcements from the main camp on the evening of the 9th.

At the Vakeel's request we sent two of
our prisoners to be examined by him at
Birti, he thinking that he would get more
information out of them than we could.
His report practically confirmed Slade's :
he estimated the numbers present at 2000,
and the killed at 700.   He expressed his
opinion that we should meet with no more
opposition till we reached Berber.

The prisoners also said that they had

heard there were 2000 men under Hassan
Wad Mahommed at Abu Hamed, consisting
of Ababdeh and Robatab men, and men
from Berber. They had converted the Government *shoona* (grain-store) into a barrack:
it is in the middle of the town, five hundred
yards from the river, and has a mud wall
ten to twelve feet high, and two feet thick.
They had constructed no other defences.

A spy who had been sent from Korti to
Berber arrived in our camp, according to
his orders, on his way back to Korti. He
had left Berber about a week before. This
was his account of the state of affairs there.
The guns which had been on the left bank
at Robush had been removed—one to Metemmeh, and one to the right bank at Berber. Mohammed el Kheir had moved his
own property across the river to the right
bank. Many Berber men had been killed
in the fight at Abu Klea, and the news of
that fight had spread terror through the
town. Most of the men now at Berber
were Magrafaab Jaalins. The Hadendowas

and the Bisharin Arabs from the Atbara had been asked to come and fight the English, but had refused. Nour Anga, the governor of Metemmeh, had sent to the Mahdi for ammunition, but it had been refused to him. The gun at Berber was out of order. Food was scarce in Berber, and the spy professed himself convinced that, when the English approached, the Jaalins between Berber and Metemmeh would surrender.

By this time I had learnt by experience that native reports might generally be classed under two heads: those of spies, who said what they thought we should like to hear; and those of professed deserters, which were intended to frighten us. We had constantly heard from our spies that the tribes were frightened; that the Mahdi's troops were deserting him; that this tribe and that had refused to join him; that the enemy would not fight, but join us when we advanced. Of these this spy's account was a specimen. We as constantly

M

heard from men who came to us, professing to be deserters, greatly exaggerated accounts of the enemy's numbers and determination to fight. Of these, the deserter who had come in to our camp at Mishami was a specimen. In fact, the only information of value was what our own reconnaissance told us, and what was supplied to us through Colvile by the Vakeel.

That evening Colonel Butler rode back to my camp, bringing with him an Arabic document. It had been found, he told me, by a private of the Cornwalls in the saddle-bag of a donkey, which was found grazing on the bank near the Kirbekan camp. There being a very strict column-order that all papers of every description found anywhere were to be preserved and sent to the intelligence officer, this paper had been kept for that purpose. But in the meantime it had been shown to the interpreter of the battalion, and rumour had spread through the camp that Khartoum had been taken and Gordon killed.

I sent for my interpreter and translator, who spoke and wrote French but not English. On my showing him the paper, and asking him what it contained, he answered : "Très mauvaises nouvelles; il dit que le Mahdi a pris Khartoum, et que Gordon a été tué." I made him translate it, and from his translation I again made the following version, which I at once sent to Abu Dom to be telegraphed to Lord Wolseley :—

Copy of a letter received from the Governor-General of Berber to the Governor of the Section.

"In the name of God, &c., from Mohammed el Kheir, Abdullah Khogeali, Emir-General of Berber, to his friend, Abdul Majid Wad el Lekalik, and all his men.—I inform you that to-day after the mid-day prayer we received a letter from the faithful Khalife Abdullah Eben Mohammed, in which he tells us that Khartoum was taken on Monday the ninth Rabi 1302, on the side of El Hauoi, in the following manner. The Mahdi (pray upon (*priez sur*) him, his dervishes, and his troops) advanced against the fortifications, and entered Khartoum in a quarter of an hour. They killed the traitor (*le perfide*) Gordon, and captured the steamers and boats. God has made him glorious; be grateful, and thank and praise God for His unspeakable mercy. I announce it to you. Tell your troops."

The document was dated the thirteenth Rabi, and on it was written, "Received, Friday the twentieth Rabi."

Comparing these dates with the 'Soudan Almanac' prepared in the Intelligence Department in London, we found that the letter announced the fall of Khartoum to have taken place on Monday the 26th January; it had been written at Berber on the 30th January, and received at the Shukook pass on Friday the 6th February. Now we understood why the enemy had returned on that day to Kirbekan, and what had stiffened their courage.

12th Feb. On the 12th the wing of the Cornwalls at Kirbekan camp advanced about a mile through the rapids to the mouth of a broad wady—probably one of the many branches of the Wady el Argu, which runs across the desert from Kirbekan to Abu Egli, on

the Nile above Berber; and the wing at
Dulka camp closed up upon them, the last
boat arriving at 4 P.M. It would have been
impossible to advance a whole battalion
farther, and it was not desirable to move
a small force in boats into the rocky
reaches of the Shukook until those reaches
were examined, and the pass itself reconnoitred to its farthest end, so that we might
ascertain what lay behind, and whether the
pass itself was clear. We were evidently
now about to become entangled in a long
rocky pass both by road and river.

The Engineers and royal naval boat,
with two sections of field-hospital, accompanied the Cornwalls. The Staffords closed
up at Kirbekan; and three companies succeeded in reaching Wady el Argu camp,
but not till very late. Five companies,
with two companies Black Watch, remained
at Kirbekan, and the Gordons closed up to
our camp opposite Dulka island. Owing
to the shallowness of the water, and their
boats being very heavily laden, they had

been obliged to abandon three boats on their way up from Hamdab.

Alleyne reconnoitred a mile and a half up stream, from Wady el Argu to the foot of a very swift rapid, which he reported must be tracked up; and Butler reconnoitred with the mounted troops, making a wide cast out into the desert, and returning through the Shukook pass, without finding any signs of the enemy. He found a site for a camp at the mouth of a wady in the Shukook pass, not far from Jebel Shukook, the mountain which is the one conspicuous feature in the mass of rugged rocks here piled together, and returned to the bivouac at Wady el Argu. Orders were therefore issued for an advance to the Shukook camp on the following day.

In the morning I had received a telegram, addressed to General Earle by the Chief of the Staff, dated the 9th. It informed me that the Government had decided that we were to stay in the Soudan till the Mahdi's power at Khartoum was

destroyed. If we could not do this before
the hot weather, we must wait until autumn.
Buller had left Gakdul on the 8th for
Gubat, and would take Metemmeh as soon
as the Royal Irish reached Gubat. It was
assumed that I could reach Berber on the
28th February, or have reported my proximity to it. Buller would be in the neighbourhood, with four or six guns and about
1500 men, on the left bank. If I did not
think I could reach Berber by that date,
I was to name a date, in order that Buller
might meet me and co-operate in the attack
on Berber. The desert road to Gubat
would be held, and a garrison left there,
with a view to subsequent operations of the
united columns against Khartoum, if, as all
native report declared to be the case, Gordon was still holding out. I was therefore
to push forward with all possible speed com-
patible with safety. I was to leave a garrison of 200 men at Abu Hamed, instead of
300 as previously ordered, with 250 rounds
of ammunition per man, and sixty days'

provisions. The telegram further contained orders as to the precautions to be taken by the commandant of the garrison, and other matters not necessary to detail.

To this telegram I replied that I did not think it possible to reach Berber by the 28th February, and that any date given must be pure conjecture, the time being dependent upon condition of unknown rapids and unknown movements of the enemy. I said it was impossible to pass more than one battalion a-day through the rapids here; and if the enemy were holding the Shukook, I must again concentrate the whole or part of my force. When we reached Salamat, I should be able to give an approximate date for reaching Abu Hamed, and at that place an approximate date for reaching Berber. Now I could only say I did not think we could reach the latter place under one month from this date (12th February). I intended to cross over my mounted troops and transport before reaching Abu Hamed.

Fresh supplies of boat-repairing material arrived during the day, sent by camel from Korti; they were very urgently needed. Our boats were suffering severely from the shallow and rocky rapids up which they had to be forced. Planks, pitch, paint, and copper nails were conspicuous by their absence; and where a plank was stove in, it had to be repaired by a patch of tin from a biscuit-box, nailed over the leak with iron nails taken from the boxes which contained our food.

Three men of the Staffords died to-day of their wounds. The other wounded of the Staffords had been carried on in their boats, arrangements having been made for their transport, and for the transport of the wounded of the Black Watch by their own regiments. Each wounded man had his boat's number attached to his stretcher, and a medical officer superintended his being placed in the boat. They were to sleep in the boats or in tents pitched on shore, as the surgeon might think best in each case.

In the first instance, the stretchers were placed athwart-ships near the stern, in front of the coxswain; but it was found that the ends of the stretchers were liable to be knocked against in hauling the boats up rapids, or coming in to shore in swift water; and as this annoyed men made nervous by pain and weakness, arrangements were afterwards made for laying the stretchers along fore and aft, on the thwarts, between the rowers. Awnings were spread for wounded men, but were not allowed in any other boats.

We had captured about 140 rifles on the scene of the action, of which the majority had been broken at the time. These broken ones we threw into the middle of the river; but about 40 Remingtons we retained, with the intention of arming our unarmed men with them in case of need; and at our request the Vakeel returned to us 1000 rounds of Remington ammunition, which we had captured at Birti, and handed over to him.

On the 13th the Cornwalls and four com- panies of the Staffords advanced about five miles, partly through rapids, to the Shukook camp. The rest of the Staffords, the Gordons, and two companies Black Watch, closed up at Wady el Argu, to which I advanced my headquarters.

Alleyne reconnoitred four miles of clear and not very swift water beyond. Through overhanging rocky cliffs, Butler, with the mounted troops, reconnoitred to the upper end of the Shukook pass opposite Uss island. Here there was another rapid, but not so formidable as some we had passed. He reported the country opening out, but no traces of cultivation; and considered that the Cornwalls and the wing of the Staffords from Shukook could reach the foot of the rapid next day, and possibly commence its passage.

The early morning saw the death of Captain Lord Avonmore from enteric fever. He, no less than those who fell at Kirbekan, was killed in action. He had overtaxed his apparently boundless energy; and the exhaustion produced by incessant exposure to the sun, and great physical fatigue, left him too weak to repel the insidious attack of the disease. We laid him by the side of the officers whom we had buried on the 10th; and as we turned away for the last time from those nameless graves, many a strong man's eyes were moist, and many a lip quivered from heartfelt emotion.

To-day the news reached us by telegram from Korti that Sir Charles Wilson and Lieutenant Stuart Wortley had reached Korti on the 9th, with a short account of Lord Charles Beresford's brilliant affair with the enemy. We learnt that half the West Kent Regiment was to leave for Gakdul on the 10th, and that Lord Wolseley would possibly leave for the same place on the 15th.

No information had yet been given to the troops as to the fall of Khartoum; but as the Reuter's telegram which arrived simultaneously with this news alluded to it as a fact established, I thought it desirable, to prevent wild rumours, to circulate the following memorandum throughout the force :—

"From information received from Lord Wolseley, there is reason to fear that the original object of this expedition—namely, the relief of General Gordon—cannot be carried out.

"When Sir Charles Wilson arrived before Khartūm, he found it in the hands of the enemy; and from information derived from a letter captured after the action of Kirbekan, it is believed that Khartūm was taken by the Mahdi on the 26th of January, and that General Gordon was killed.

"Sir Charles Wilson in returning from Khartūm was wrecked. He and his party appear to have taken refuge on an island, whence, according to information received from the Chief of the Staff, they were brought off by a steamer under the command of Captain Lord Charles Beresford, R.N.

"Lord Charles Beresford had a brilliant little engagement with the enemy, who were in position on the bank with four guns. One shot hit the boiler, disabling the steamer till the boiler was repaired, which was done under fire, taking the greater part of the day. One sailor was killed, and Lieutenant Van Koughnet, R.N., wounded, but not dangerously.

"Sir Charles Wilson and Lieutenant Stuart Wortley arrived at Korti on the night of the 10th instant.

"It is understood to be the present intention of her Majesty's Government to break up the Mahdi's power in the Soudan, and a strong force of all arms is proceeding to Souakim to crush Osman Digna.

"Headquarters and three companies of the West Kent Regiment left Korti on the 10th instant for Gakdul.

"Lord Wolseley will probably leave later to join General Buller's force, and co-operate with this column in the capture of Berber."

14th Feb.   On the 14th the Cornwalls advanced to and reached the foot of Uss rapid, opposite Little Uss island, entered the rapid, and made some progress through it.   Here was the true upper entrance to the Shukook pass, which had evidently been the site of a camp of the enemy.   I halted the leading wing of the Staffords at the foot of the rapid, and the Gordons and other wing of the Staffords closed up upon them before nightfall. The Black Watch reached Wady el Argu, as did the artillery and convoy.

I moved my headquarters to the foot of Uss rapid. The troopers sent back as guides by Colonel Butler to lead me from our Wady el Argu camp through the Shukook, instead of turning to the right, as they should have done, at the entrance to the pass, took a turn to the left, and involved me and the baggage-convoy in a labyrinth of the wildest description.

The path by which they brought us was utterly unfitted for a track for loaded camels, though practicable enough for horses. We marched for six miles through as bad ground as it was possible to traverse, wedged in between rocks; and it was evidently impossible that this could be what was after all a well-known and much-travelled pass. Inquiries from Abu Bekr, who was in rear with the baggage, satisfied me that there was another road far better, and little, if at all, longer; and I sent back Colonel Colvile

with Abu Bekr to Wady el Argu, to lead
the convoy by the better route the next day.

Colonel Butler reconnoitred three or four
miles beyond the head of Uss rapid, and
found swift water but no bad rapid.   Cultivation commenced ahead; and there were
many mimosa-trees, the ground becoming
more open.   No signs of any enemy, and
all inhabitants fled.

A spy returned from Salamat, which was
now only ten miles from our advanced camp,
reported that the people had fled on the 12th,
carrying all their possessions with them, in
the direction of the Robatab country or into
the desert.   Colonel Butler was therefore instructed to push his mounted troops home
into Salamat the following day, and ascertain whether it was still held by the enemy
or not.

I was now in a position to place the
Gordon Highlanders ahead of the Staffordshire Regiment in the order of march, and
accordingly the following orders were issued
for the next day's advance :—

" The Cornwalls to continue their advance through Uss rapid, covered by the advance of the mounted troops ; the Gordons to enter the Uss rapid, moving in two columns—one by each bank ; the Staffords to be in readiness to follow the Gordons ; the Black Watch to advance from Wady el Argu to the foot of Uss rapid."

This rapid opposite Uss island, though not marked in any map or mentioned in any account of the river, proved one of the most troublesome obstacles we had yet encountered. Boats had to track singly by the island bank up the last rush of water. The Gordons had passed through the lower 15th Feb. portion of the rapid, and closed up on the rear of the Cornwalls, long before these were all through the upper rush of water. In fact, by 2 P.M. only the Cornwalls and two companies of the Gordons were through the rapid.

Meanwhile Butler reconnoitred with the mounted troops, and at 1.30 P.M. entered the beginning of the long village of Sala-

N

mat, which extends for some two and a half miles along the left bank opposite the island of Sherri.   He found the whole village deserted.   He reported that there was another bad rapid opposite Sherari island — but above that, clear water apparently for some miles; and that opposite the upper end of the village of Salamat, the yellow sand of the true right bank of the Nile was again visible.

Alleyne, with the leading boats, reached a small village opposite the island of Shoar, about four miles above the Uss rapid, in four hours from leaving the head of the rapid, and halted there.   All boats which had passed through the Uss rapid by 2 P.M., and which could therefore reach the Shoar bivouac before dark, were sent on there.

The remainder of the Gordons were passed through Uss rapid, and encamped on the left bank at its head.   The Staffords concentrated on a small sand island at the foot of the bad part of the rapid, ready to commence passing through it at daylight;

and the Black Watch bivouacked in the
camp at the foot, occupied by the Staffords
and Gordons the preceding night.

Early in the day I had moved my headquarters to the old dervish's camp opposite
to the rapid and to the entrance of the
Shukook pass, and about noon had the
pleasure of seeing the head of the convoy
and the battery emerge from the pass. That
pass had long been a subject of anxiety to
us, and rightly so. In the course of the
day I rode back some two or three miles
through it, and an uglier place it was difficult to conceive. In some places there
was barely room for a loaded camel to
pass between the perpendicular rocks; in
others, where the path was wider, the rocks
had been prepared for defence by loopholed
stone sconces, in the same way as the koppies and ridge at Kirbekan. There was
no order or regularity in the plan of the
rocks. They seemed to have been up-
heaved as a mass in some great volcanic
convulsion, and to have fallen one upon

another in every direction, covering a space
some six miles long by three or four broad.
With our infantry tied to the boats, as it
was, and with so small a force of mounted
troops, it would have been a most difficult
task to dislodge an active and determined
enemy from such a position, of which he
knew every outlet, and of which we knew
nothing.   It was an oppressive place to
remain in.   It had not even the redeeming
element of grandeur, such as great massive
features give to the most rugged mountain-
range.   It represented low, sullen savagery.
It was typical of the tribe to whom it
belonged.

Orders were issued for a general advance
of all the boats from their respective positions in the morning; and I was enabled,
with a light heart, to report to Lord Wolseley that our cavalry had entered Salamat,
and that the convoy was through the Shukook pass.

CHAPTER XI.

SALAMAT—DESTRUCTION OF SULEIMAN WAD GAMR'S PROPERTY.

MY report to Lord Wolseley on the 15th was 15th Feb. to the following effect: "Cavalry entered Salamat to - day, and found it deserted. Leading infantry are within five miles of Salamat; but a bad rapid intervenes oppo- site Sherari island, which will probably require 500 yards' portage. The rapid opposite Uss island is not marked in any map, nor had we any information of its existence; but it takes three days to get the troops through it. Under conditions of exceptionally low Nile and unexpected rapids, any estimate of time must be mere guess - work. I hope I may reach Abu

Hamed in ten days, but do not think I can concentrate there in less than fourteen, as I have all my camels and horses to cross over."

Colonel Butler, in his reconnaissance of the 15th, had reported Sherri island as being richly cultivated, with many houses. Some of the inhabitants had hailed his party across the river, and asked for "grace," exactly in the same way as the inhabitants of Hebbeh had asked for "grace" from Colonel Stewart when his steamer was wrecked there. Butler had replied that grace would be given to all except the murderers of Stewart and his companions; and the islanders replied that they had to consult the rest of their people, and would reply when all our soldiers had arrived at Salamat.

16th Feb. On the 16th the mounted troops advanced and covered the head of Sherari rapid, while the Cornwalls advanced to it and succeeded in passing six companies through, which bivouacked above the rapid.

The lower half of this rapid was not difficult when once the channel was known; but there was only one narrow and difficult passage through the upper half. In one place there was only just sufficient water through sunken rocks for a hundred yards. The boats were all taken through by a party of voyageurs. A company of the Gordons, with Captain Peel, was sent to try another channel round Sherari island; but they returned, having lost one boat swamped. The remainder of the Cornwalls and the Gordons bivouacked below the upper portion of the rapid—the Staffords at Shoar, and the Black Watch still at Uss—the river above being too much blocked with boats for them to move during the day. The mounted troops joined the Cornwalls at the head of the rapid. Headquarters bivouacked with the Gordons; and the convoy was brought on to the same place, as it afforded good camping-ground and forage.

In consequence of the attitude of the inhabitants of Sherri island, I sent to them a letter in Arabic, promising that if they would lay down their arms and assist us with supplies, no one should be harmed except the murderers of Colonel Stewart, and that their houses and *sakyehs* should be spared. The letter was delivered on the island.

Orders were issued for all troops to advance on the following day—the cavalry to cover the advance of the Cornwalls; the camel corps to remain in bivouac, and cover the convoy, artillery, and troops in the Sherari cataract.

17th Feb. On the 17th, Colonel Butler, with the cavalry, occupied Salamat by 9 A.M., and at the same hour two companies of the Cornwalls landed on Sherri island. They found it deserted, and commenced to search for supplies. No cattle were found, but a considerable quantity of grain and dates, which, together with a supply of grain found on Uss island, completed the loads of our camel transport to its full carrying power.

The Sherari cataract caused great delay

and considerable damage to boats. The Staffords and the Gordons each lost one boat, damaged beyond repair; but no lives were lost. By sunset the Cornwalls and three companies of the Gordons were in bivouac at Salamat, with the naval boat, Engineers, part of the field-hospital, and the cavalry. Headquarters also moved to Salamat, and occupied a house in a walled garden near the river-bank, belonging to a sister of Abu Bekr—an aunt, therefore, of Suleiman Wad Gamr. All the camel troops and convoy advanced to a good camping-ground, with ample forage, at the head of Sherari. Colonel Butler reconnoitred as far as Jebel Asma, and ascended the mountain. He reported clear water for nine miles from Salamat, no trace of enemy, and signs of cultivation along the river-bank beyond Jebel Asma.

The infantry continued their slow progress through the rapids. The remainder of the Gordons and the Staffords bivouacked at Sherari, and the Black Watch at Shoar.

On the previous evening a telegram from the acting Chief of the Staff had arrived, dated 13th, giving projects for sending us up supplies by hired camels, and stating what supplies we might possibly find at Abu Hamed. It informed me that a convoy was to start from Korosko on the 15th, which should reach Abu Hamed by the 20th or 21st; that Lord Wolseley anticipated that I could be ready to leave Abu Hamed on the 22d or 23d; but as he could not let me leave it until he should hear from General Buller, I was to await orders there, and he scarcely hoped I should reach Berber until the 13th or 14th March.

The telegram informed me of Lord Wolseley's proposals for the disposition of the troops after the projected capture of Berber, and of my own share, and that of my column, in these arrangements; but as subsequent events made these proposals void, it is not necessary to reproduce them here.

Captain Kekewich, D.A.A.G., also arrived with despatches, having left Korti on the

13th, and travelled through by camel in three days from Abu Dom. He brought me a letter from Lord Wolseley, and a copy of the instructions to General Buller, dated 12th February. With him returned from Abu Dom all the camel-corps men hitherto employed in carrying messages to and from that place,—arrangements having now been made with the commandant at Abu Dom, and the Vakeel at Birti, to supply messengers between these places, and with the latter to supply messengers from Birti to our camp. From Captain Keke-wich we learned something of the situation on the desert side, so far as it was known at Korti up to the date of his leaving.

I replied to-day to the Chief of the Staff's telegram. I said frankly that I had no faith in the promises of any sheikhs that they would forward supplies to our camp, and that the convoy I was to receive at Abu Hamed from Korosko would enable my force to live till the 23d April, and no longer. I entered into questions of supply as affecting Lord Wolseley's proposed plan of operations, expressed my fears as to too sanguine an estimate having been formed both as to time and supplies, and again repeated that I could fix no dates, rate of progress being dependent on unknown conditions. I informed him that my rear battalion could only reach Salamat on the 19th.

Immediately on arrival at Salamat, Suleiman Wad Gamr's house had been taken possession of and searched. Many relics of the murder were found there, including one of poor Stewart's visiting-cards stained with blood, extracts from M. Herbin's papers, and photographs of M. Herbin and of the Austrian consul, presented by them to Mr Power. Chests of papers were found here, and great numbers of papers, with some few relics of the murder, on Sherri island. All these were secured and carefully examined by the interpreters; and orders were issued for all the troops at Salamat, except the pickets and a search-party ordered to Sherri island, to parade under the intelligence officers with axes, picks, and shovels, for the destruction of property.   The other troops were ordered to close up to Salamat.

On the 18th the Gordons and Staffords 18th Feb. closed up on the Cornwalls at Salamat. The damaged boats of the Cornwalls and Gordons were repaired, the repairing party working till late.   The Black Watch entered, and a portion passed through, the Sherari cataract.

The foraging party on Sherri island was successful, and brought over some forty camel-loads of grain in their boats.   The troops were, I fear, much disappointed at not obtaining permission to destroy the houses and *sakyehs* on the island; but knowing that sooner or later we should have to return down the river, I forbade all destruction which, without any marked object to be gained, would interfere with the sources of supply on our return.   The discipline of the troops was admirable.   At one time some unauthorised burning of huts had taken place—not, I believe, by enlisted soldiers.

I had therefore published an order absolutely forbidding such irregularities, directing
that any soldier, voyageur, or interpreter,
plundering or setting fire to any house,
sakyeh, or trees, without authority, was to
be tried by summary court-martial, and
pointing out that the offence was punishable
with death. From that date the offence
entirely ceased.

The troops had set to with a will to
destroy Suleiman Wad Gamr's property.
His house was a large one, standing on an
eminence, with a colonnade supported by
pillars, and several courtyards, each with
several rooms. Roofs were pulled down,
all wood available for firewood carried off,
the walls shaken by charges of gun-cotton,
and then utterly destroyed by the pick and
the shovel. Beams and solid wooden doors,
rare articles in this country, were destroyed
by fire, and the house was razed to the
ground. All his *sakyehs* were burnt, and
his palm-trees were cut down and destroyed
with fire.

By way of instruction, I ordered a wing of the Staffords to occupy Sheikh Omar's house as their bivouac this evening, and to place it in a defensible state, with orders to destroy it and the rest of Omar's property in the morning—Omar having escaped from the Vakeel, and rejoined Suleiman. Abu Bekr's property and that of his sister were spared.

These houses were of a higher class than any we had met with in the Shagiyeh or Monassir country. They had some attempt at ornament, and stood in gardens. In Abu Bekr's garden there was an orange-tree full of blossom, the only one we had seen since leaving Dongola.

Colvile's soldier-servant came into camp to-day, having had a curious adventure. He and a native servant of Colvile's, a Dongolese or Shagiyeh—I forget which—having left the bivouac of the previous day on camels with Colvile's baggage for Salamat, had taken a wrong turn in a wady, and had strayed into the desert, where they lost themselves and wandered about till nightfall, without water, and with little food. In the early morning they started to try and find the camp, and came upon a party of natives—doubtless nomad Monassir— tending cattle in a wady, with their women and children. The native servant asserted that they invited him to join them in killing the white man, but he told them there were 50,000 English at Salamat, who had come here on purpose to avenge another Englishman's death, and they would certainly all be killed if they hurt this one. At all events the two servants were shown their way to Salamat, and allowed to proceed unharmed, —another tolerably convincing proof of the moral effect of the fight at Kirbekan.

Butler reconnoitred four or five miles beyond Jebel Asma, reported the river clear, the country fairly open, and ample cultivation for foraging herds of animals. Orders were therefore issued for the advance to recommence in the morning, the Cornwalls leading, followed by the Gordons; the

Staffords to halt at Salamat, repair their
boats, and demolish Sheikh Omar's property.   The Black Watch, battery, and
convoy, to close up to Salamat.   The
cavalry to cover the advance with half the
camel corps and two guns.

Reporting the intended advance to the
Chief of the Staff to-day, I said: " I am un-
willing to send back soldiers with messages,
and native runners are limited in number.
I shall therefore not attempt to communicate with you again after this, unless something special occurs, until I reach Abu
Hamed, which I hope to do about 26th
instant."

A native taken prisoner by our scouts
stated he had left Abu Hamed four days
ago, and had met crowds of men, women,
and children, with cattle and camels, making
their way up the river on both banks.   He
said they had few rifles, but many spears;
and he had heard that Suleiman Wad
Gamr was retiring on Berber, by order of
Mohammed el Kheir.   All the Monassir

o

villages were deserted, but the Robatab villages were still inhabited.

19th Feb. On the 19th the advance from Salamat commenced. Omar's house was razed to the ground, and his *sakyehs* and palm-trees destroyed. A quantity of grain was collected. The cavalry and camel troops started with grain for six days; every transport camel was fully loaded up, and the camels had a good feed. The last of the troops and the convoy closed up at Salamat, and were ordered to advance on the following day.

CHAPTER XII.

HEBBEH—THE PASSAGE OF THE NILE.

ON the 19th, Colonel Butler on the bank, 19th Feb. and Colonel Alleyne in his boat, recon- noitred for a distance of between eleven and twelve miles from Salamat, and Butler selected a site for a bivouac at Sulimanyeh, about nine miles above Salamat, and about two and a half miles below the wreck of Stewart's steamer; and the Cornwalls, Gor- dons, and details concentrated there by five o'clock. Butler reported that when he ar- rived opposite the wreck, two Arab scouts on camels began to shout from the right bank, and then rode off to the north. We had seen the enemy's scouts in the same way on our arrival at Salamat. A prisoner taken

beyond the site of the wreck asserted that
Suleiman Wad Gamr had arrived at Sulimanyeh on the 16th, and had gone northwards
on the 17th, taking with him Fakri Wad
Etman; he was said to be accompanied
by about 400 men and a number of women
and children, with many cattle, camels, donkeys, and much baggage. Lekalik, with
the force which had retreated from the
Shukook pass, was said to have preceded
Suleiman Wad Gamr, two of the sheikhs
that had been with him at the Shukook
having been sent direct to Berber.

Another prisoner informed us that he
had left the neighbourhood of Abu Hamed
on the 14th. He heard that many men
from Berber had arrived there, and that
there were 2000 Ababdehs, 1000 Bisharin,
and some Robatab assembled there to
defend Abu Hamed.

Although the accounts of prisoners were
by no means to be trusted, there was a
persistency in the accounts of the flights
along the left bank which, coupled with the

hasty and complete abandonment of the
Shukook pass, led me to believe that the
enemy in front of us was in a state of
demoralisation, and unlikely to make any
stand.   On the other hand, the presence of
the enemy's mounted scouts on the right
bank—their defiant attitude as they retired,
menacing us by voice and gesture, as the
enemy's outposts on the left bank had men-
aced us before Kirbekan, but at no other
time—led me to believe the consistent reports that on the right bank at, or possibly
before reaching, Abu Hamed, we should
meet with a more determined opposition, in
which it was probable the news of the fall
of Khartoum might induce both Ababdeh
and Bisharin Arabs to join.

I was therefore anxious to cross my
mounted troops and transport animals over
to the right bank as soon as practicable, and
resolved to do this at the first convenient
locality.   Little was to be gained by advancing farther on the left bank ; for though
there was perhaps more cultivation on it

than on the right bank, both were barren
sandy wastes, with only occasional patches
of growing crops; and as at Sulimanyeh we
were within little more than forty miles of
Abu Hamed, and all accounts united in
agreeing that there was but one more rapid
of any importance—that close to Mograt
island — the time before reaching Abu
Hamed should now be so brief, that a little
better grazing for the camels did not weigh
against the importance of effecting the
crossing without opposition.

I had attached Colonel Colvile to the
advanced guard under Butler since his
arrival in camp after guiding the convoy
through the Shukook, with instructions to
send in a sketch daily to accompany Colonel
Butler's report. Judging from his sketch
received this evening at Salamat that a
favourable crossing - place would be found
near Sulimanyeh, I wrote to Colonel Butler
saying that the whole of the troops at Salamat would move to Sulimanyeh on the 20th,
that I should myself start at 7 and be in

his camp at 8.30, and that I begged him to
wait for me there.   He was to send on the
Cornwalls and Gordons in the morning by
river, but not the guns or any baggage or
baggage-animals till after my arrival; and
two companies of each of the leading battalions were to halt on the left bank opposite to Hebbeh, with all the axes, picks,
and shovels the battalions could furnish.
No troops were to be allowed to land on
the right bank.   My intention was, if
there was a favourable crossing-place at
Sulimanyeh, to cross all the animals and
guns over there with the boats of the two
rear battalions, to visit and examine the
site of Stewart's murder, and then destroy
the house and surrounding property of
Fakri Wad Etman.   If there should not be
a favourable crossing-place, the dispositions
were such that no delay whatever would be
caused.

On the morning of the 20th I reached 20th Feb.
Sulimanyeh at the hour named, and told
Colonel Butler my views.   He said that

Hebbeh itself afforded so favourable a site for
the crossing, that he had directed Alleyne
to halt all the boats there, pending my decision. On arrival opposite Hebbeh, directly
opposite the wrecked steamer, I found all
the conditions for a favourable crossing
fulfilled. On this side a high commanding
bank, with clear view over the neighbouring
country, affording an excellent position for
infantry and guns both to sweep the opposite bank and hold their own against any
attack from this side. Below the high bank,
but easily approached by a natural ramp, a
long sandbank sloping gradually into the
water. On the opposite side, but a quarter
of a mile below, a high Nile island, forming
a strong position for infantry, and with a
similar sandbank—the breadth from the left
bank to the high Nile island being about
300 yards. The high Nile island itself was
separated from the right bank only by a
narrow channel, over which at one place
there was a dry crossing.

I at once ordered the crossing to be

undertaken. Sending the Cornwalls over in their boats to establish themselves on the high Nile island, and to take up a position to cover the crossing, and bringing half the Gordons to the high ground on the left bank, where I directed them to form a zareeba, I sent back orders to Sulimanyeh for the guns and baggage there to be brought on by their escort, and for the whole of the troops and convoy on their arrival there, both by land and water, to be pushed on to Hebbeh.

We could see with our glasses that we were being watched from behind the sand-hills less than a mile out in the desert on the right bank, and Butler at once crossed over with a scouting-party of Hussars, before whom the enemy's scouts retired. About 11 A.M. the baggage of the advanced guard and two guns arrived from Sulimanyeh, and the guns were at once placed in position. Our Hussars formed a line of vedettes on a radius of a mile and a half from the point of crossing on the left bank, and those first sent across placed vedettes in commanding positions about a mile out on the right bank. About the same hour, 11 A.M., the leading boats of the Black Watch and Staffords arrived. They had advanced along both banks from Salamat. By one o'clock the remainder of the battery and the convoy arrived, under escort of half the camel corps.

The troops and baggage were crossed over in the following order :—

Scouting-party 19th Hussars.

Support, consisting of half the camel corps.

Two guns of the Egyptian battery, with their camels—having been replaced in their position on the left bank by the four remaining guns on their arrival; they were placed in position on high Nile island as soon as crossed over.

Cavalry baggage.

Camel corps baggage.

Remainder of the 19th Hussars—having been relieved on vedette duty by the half of the camel corps which had escorted the convoy.

Camels of the four guns on the left bank.

Headquarter baggage and horses, and infantry regimental horses.

The transport company, camels, and loads.

The cattle and donkeys.

The four guns.

Remaining half of the camel corps.

Each animal was towed over by a boat, —its saddle, load, and driver or rider being, as a rule, ferried across in that boat. The ferrying commenced at 11 A.M. and ended for the day at 5.30 P.M., recommenced at 7 A.M. and finished at 2 P.M., having thus occupied thirteen and a half hours of actual work, during which time 780 animals, with their equipment and loads, and their drivers or riders, and six guns, had been taken across.

20th to 21st Feb.

The crossing was effected under the superintendence of Colonel Alleyne, as-

sisted by all the staff officers available.
Two crossing-places were worked at the
same time; and it was found that as many
as fifty boats could be simultaneously employed, but not more. The crossing was
made down-stream, the actual distance traversed being about 400 yards.

The water being too shallow for the
boats to come quite up to the dry shore of
the sandbank, each animal, having had a
rope fastened securely round its head by
one of Lieutenant Bourke's blue-jackets, or
by one of the Egyptian camel-men, was
led into the water, and the loose end of
the rope was handed to a man in the stern.
The boat was then rowed off from shore,
and the animal followed till out of its
depth, when it commenced to swim, or, in
some cases of camels, lay on its side and
allowed itself to be towed across. The
horses swam freely; and it was found important to let them have ample length of
rope, with their heads freed from any
strain. With the camels, on the other

hand, it was found necessary to have a very short rope, and to hold the animal's head well above water, close up to the boat. The camel is an indifferent swimmer. He can make his way down-stream for a short time, but soon becomes exhausted; and he cannot swim against a strong stream. The tendency always is for his head to go under, and his hindquarters to rise above the water; and the Egyptian artillerymen counteracted this by sitting astride on the rumps of their camels, thus forcing the quarters down, when the heads correspondingly rise. The camels which were least exhausted were those that lay on their sides, and, with their heads held well up close to the hands of the man in the stern, allowed themselves, thus suspended, to be towed across without attempting to swim.

The veterinary surgeon with his assistants was stationed on the right bank, and administered restoratives to any animals which appeared exhausted on arrival. I have noticed, for future guidance, that the points chiefly to be attended to, in addition to the length of rope above-mentioned, are the tying of the head-rope, great care being necessary to prevent its slipping or getting round the animal's nostrils; the hours of crossing, which should not be very early or very late, but when the sun is well up, so that there is less risk of chill; the pace of the boats, which, in the case of horses and camels, should be regulated by their pace of swimming; immediate administration of restoratives to exhausted animals; and gentle exercise after crossing for all.

We lost only three camels. One, the rope having broken, floated down the rapid water and was drowned. Two died from suffocation, the rope having slipped and closed their nostrils. Six others, nearly all from among those which crossed over late in the evening, suffered subsequently from epileptic fits, similar to staggers in a horse.

Of these, three recovered, and the rest died; though had they been able to rest for a few days, they also would in all probability have recovered. No casualty occurred among the horses or cattle. One donkey died of exhaustion.

CHAPTER XIII.

HEBBEH—THE SCENE OF COLONEL STEWART'S MURDER.

20th to 21st Feb. WHILE the crossing was in progress on the 20th, I visited the wreck and the scene of the murder, taking with me those of the staff who could be spared, and the commanding officers of regiments. We found the steamer impaled on a large rock, about two hundred yards from the proper right bank of the river. She was a much larger vessel than we had supposed her to be. She was seventy feet in length from stem to stern, and twenty-two feet in breadth over her paddles : the depth of her hold was four feet six inches. Plates of iron a quarter of an inch thick protected her sides,

pitted with bullet-marks, and torn through
in places by case-shot or splinters of shell.
She lay with her keel sixteen feet above
the present level of the water, in a channel
studded with rocks—an intricate narrow
labyrinth; while on the left bank of the
river there was open clear water for nearly
three hundred yards in breadth, so that at
the time of the wreck there must have
been nearly four hundred yards of open
water on that bank. Yet her pilot had
steered her into this rocky maze, where,
even at high Nile, many of the rocks must
have shown above water. To us it seemed
incredible that the wreck was an accident,
for it was almost impossible to believe she
had not been purposely steered to her
destruction. And yet, who can say? At
high Nile she would have come rushing
down the swift water above, and a very
small error in steering would have caused
her to be swept in here.

The natives had stripped her of everything that could be of use, leaving her a

P

mere shell. All her wood-work had been carried away, including the floats of her paddles, and such iron as was sufficiently portable. The after-part of her hold was filled with sand, her bows were high out of water. A few torn scraps of letters and paper, of no particular interest, were littered about; but there was nothing whatever worth preserving as a relic.

From the steamer we walked by a dry causeway to the mainland—right bank—which we followed down-stream for about four hundred yards, when we came to the first group of houses of Hebbeh. We had brought with us Abu Bekr, the uncle of Suleiman Wad Gamr, and I have seldom seen a man in a more wholesome state of fear. He evidently thought that we had brought him here to execute him on the spot. But he mastered his terrors, and pointed out to us the house of Fakri Wad Etman. It was an ordinary native mud-house, the external entrance being into a small courtyard, on one side of which was

the house. But it was not here, Abu Bekr
told us, that the strangers would have been
received. In this house the women lived,
and no strangers would have been admitted
there. The murder must have taken place
in the *salaamlik*, or guest-chamber—a detached mud-hut of one room only, some
fifty yards from the dwelling-house. We
entered this small room, stooping to pass
under the low doorway with feelings of
awe. But there was nothing to remind us
of the terrible tragedy that had taken place
there six months before. There were no
signs of blood. The floor and all the
ground round the hut had been carefully
strewn with fine sand.

A hundred yards in front of the door, on
the river-bank, stood a group of palms, the
scene of another tragedy. But I will let
the story be told in the words of one who
was fortunate enough to escape from the
scene, as taken down from his own lips by
Major Slade, through the medium of an
interpreter, on the 1st February.

STATEMENT OF HASSEIN ISMAIN.

" I am the stoker of the steamer Abbas,
which left Khartoum about six months ago, on
a Wednesday. Stewart Pasha, two European
consuls, twelve Greeks, five artillery soldiers, four
Arab women and four slave women, and seven
native crew, were on board. The captain of the
steamer was Mahomed Saf. Eddin, and the *reises*
[pilots] Ali Bishteeli and Mohamed. Two other
steamers accompanied us to beyond Berber, and
four nuggers sailed with us, which were towed as
far as Berber by the two steamers. The steamers
shelled the forts at Berber, and when our steamer
was safely past, they left us, and we continued
our journey with the four nuggers. We left the
nuggers behind us, just before reaching Abu
Hamed, and steamed on.

" On a Thursday, three days before the end of
the month of Dhul-kadeh [18th September], at
about nine in the morning, the steamer ran on
a rock about two feet below the surface in Wad
Gamr's country. Before we struck we had seen
several people running away into the hills on
both banks. When we struck, the small boat
was filled with our things, and everything was
landed on the small island. Four trips were
made between the steamer and the island, and
when everything of value had been landed,

Stewart Pasha returned to the steamer himself, drove a nail into the vent of the gun, and filed the projecting part off. The gun was bolted to the deck of the ship, and the artillery soldiers set it free, and threw it overboard. Two boxes of gun-ammunition were also thrown overboard at the same time.

"While this was going on, several people came to the right bank and shouted out, 'Give us peace and grace.' Hassan Bey, belonging to the Tele-graph Department, acted as interpreter to Stewart Pasha, and told the natives that they would have peace. Four or five natives swam over to the island, and Hassan Bey returned with them in the small boat to the right bank, and saw Sheikh Suleiman Wad Gamr, who was in a house near the bank. Hassan asked him for camels to take the party to Merawi, and Suleiman ordered four camels to be taken to the bank to be loaded with the baggage, and Hassan returned. Suleiman then sent two men to the island to invite Stewart Pasha to land and come to the house. Every-body then landed on the right bank, taking with them all the baggage. Hassan Bey then went to the house of a blind man named Etman Fakri, with two men ; and he was told by Suleiman to ask Stewart Pasha and the two consuls to come in and drink coffee, and arrange about the price to be paid for the camels. This was at about

4 P. M. The soldiers wanted to accompany Stewart Pasha as a guard ; but Hassan Bey said that it would frighten the people, and the camels would not be given.

"Stewart Pasha, the two consuls, and Hassan Bey then entered the house of Etman Fakri. They were all unarmed except Stewart Pasha, who had a small revolver on his belt. After a short time, I saw Suleiman come out of the house with a copper water-pot in his hand. He made a sign to the people who were standing about the village armed with swords and spears ; and immediately the people divided into two parties, one going to the house of Etman Fakri, and the other rushing to the place (by the palms) where the rest of Stewart's party was assembled. I was with this party, and when the natives charged us, we threw ourselves into the river. The natives fired at us and killed many ; others were drowned. I swam to a small island, and remained there till it was dark, when I swam to the left bank. I remained there for some time, and then made my way to Hamdab. There I was taken by a man called Taha Wad Fadeil, made prisoner, and taken to Sheikh Omar, uncle of Suleiman Wad Gamr, at Birti. He told me to remain with him and not escape, and he would treat me well. I have been at Birti ever since, and remained there after the dervishes ran away the day before yesterday.

"I heard that when the natives entered the house of Etman Fakri, they fell upon Stewart Pasha and the consuls, and killed them all. Hassan Bey escaped, wounded in the arm by a knife, and went to Berber. When the natives rushed into the hut, Hassan Bey held the blind man in front of him, and thus was saved. The captain was killed.

"Two of the artillery soldiers, the two *reises*, and three of the native crew, are alive at Berber. Four full-grown slaves, one woman slave, and two young ones, are also alive, and were near Birti, in the desert looking after cattle, a month ago. The money found was divided amongst the natives who fell upon the party. Everything else was sent to Berber. Two bundles of spears, and two suits of chain-armour, the property of one of the consuls, were at Birti.

"All the bodies of those murdered were thrown into the river."

We found but few traces of the murder: some fragments of books, more of poor Stewart's visiting-cards, a shirt-sleeve stained with blood, and a few papers, apparently belonging to MM. Herbin and Power. At Sherari island we had found five pages of Stewart's diary, describing Gordon's entry

into Abu Hamed and Berber on the way
from Korosko to Khartoum.

We pressed Abu Bekr as to how Suleiman Wad Gamr came to be at the scene
of the wreck, and he told us that as soon
as the steamer went ashore, Fakri Wad
Etman had sent a message to Suleiman
Wad Gamr at Salamat; and that Suleiman had immediately ordered his camels,
and had hastened to Hebbeh. This was
quite consistent with the stoker's account of
the wreck having taken place at nine, and
Suleiman's first appearance on the scene
some time in the afternoon, when Hassan
Bey went to Fakri Wad Etman's house,
after all the baggage had been removed
from the steamer, the gun spiked, and the
ammunition destroyed.

Orders were issued for the destruction of
the property of Fakri Wad Etman and the
21st Feb. village of Hebbeh on the 21st. The work
was superintended by the officers of the
Intelligence Department, who searched
everywhere for papers or relics, boring and

digging wherever the ground seemed disturbed. Some skeletons were found, but they were old, and of Africans. Little or nothing of interest was discovered. There was no trace of that journal of which Gordon spoke in such high terms. Fakri Wad Etman's houses were destroyed, his *sakyehs* burnt, and his palm-trees cut down and set on fire : his *salaamlik* was razed to the ground.

CHAPTER XIV.

HUELLA—THE END OF THE MONASSIR COUNTRY.

21st Feb. ON the night of the 21st, headquarters bivouacked on the high Nile island with the
Cornwalls and Staffords, mounted troops,
and convoy. The Gordons and Black
Watch bivouacked on the left bank. Butler
reconnoitred a few miles to the front, and
reported the river very swift for about two
miles, and then again comparatively easy.
With the exception of an occasional small
village with cultivation, the open desert of
yellow sand reached to the water's edge.

We now were about to leave the region
of rocks, and to enter a country where there
was breathing-space. The character of the
opposition likely to be encountered was also

changed. We had no longer to fear ambus-
cades in ravines, or to expect to find rocky
gorges held against us by ensconced riflemen. If the enemy on the right bank
meant battle before our reaching Abu
Hamed, he must fight us in comparatively
open ground, where the discipline of our
troops, and the superiority of our weapons,
must tell with deadly effect; and, if report
was true, we might expect here to meet the
nomad Bisharin Arabs, whose tactics would
probably be like those of the Hadendowas
at Teb and Tamai, or the enemy encountered by Herbert Stewart. The change
was a great relief; but we had also to
consider that the enemy we should now
encounter would consist of fresh troops,
undaunted by previous defeat.

The following orders were therefore issued : "In the further advance of the
column by river, every effort must be made
to keep the boats well closed up, not by
constant delays on the part of the leading
boats to wait for the remainder, but by stren-

uous exertions on the part of the crews of
the boats in rear to keep up with those leading the advance. Commanding officers will
impress upon all non-commissioned officers
and men that the success of the expedition,
and its safety while moving by river, depend
mainly upon the amount of energy which
they put into their work.

" The advance will be covered on the
right bank by the mounted troops, who will
give warning to the leading boats of any
aggressive movement of the enemy. Should
the officers commanding the mounted troops
report the enemy advancing to attack, the
leading boats will fall back on the rear boats
of the leading half-battalion, and the rear
half-battalion will close up. As soon as the
leading half battalion is concentrated, the
troops will be landed and at once formed
up to meet the attack in the strongest available position. All following battalions, unless specially ordered to the contrary, will
close up on the leading battalion, land, and
await orders."

The orders for an unexpected landing
issued by Major-General Earle on 19th
January were republished, and attention
called to their salient points. The various
departmental boats were assigned their
places in the column.

" The advance by land of the guns and
convoy, and their escort, must be guided by
circumstances," ran the order, "which may
change from day to day; therefore no pre-
cise rules can be laid down, but all transport must be kept well together, must move
on as wide a front as the nature of the
ground permits, and must invariably be protected by flankers, well thrown out into the
desert."

On the morning of the 22d the column 22d Feb.
advanced, the Gordon Highlanders leading,
at 6.45 A.M. The river immediately above
our crossing-place was very swift and difficult, and it was late in the afternoon before
the last boat was through it. Two miles of
swift and rocky water followed. The two
leading battalions and mounted troops—

under Colonel Butler—bivouacked at a
small village about six miles above Hebbeh,
and nearly opposite a remarkable rock of
white marble, standing alone in the river,
called Hajar el Baida, " the white rock."
The cavalry reconnoitred six miles to the
front, and saw no trace of the enemy.

The remainder of the column bivouacked
at El Kab, about a mile below Hajar el
Baida. Here there was a small village with
a fair quantity of growing crops. There
was also a large stone fort on a high rock
over the river, and another on the opposite
bank, of precisely the same nature as those
already spoken of at Kabenat, below Birti.
We took up a strong defensive position here,
with a company on outpost on a high detached rock in front, only accessible by one
steep path. The country beyond was flat
desert, or undulating sand-dunes.

Before moving off from Hebbeh in the
morning, I had released a spy of El Zain.
This man had been brought in by our
scouts, and after telling many different

stories, had at last confessed to being a
spy of El Zain, sent by him to obtain information of our strength and movements.
I suppose he ought to have been hanged,
but I thought he would be more useful
alive; and having extracted from him such
information as he would give as to El Zain's
position and strength, I let him see the
whole force, and then sent him back to El
Zain, bidding him tell that robber-chief
what he had seen at Kirbekan and Hebbeh.

On the 23d the boats advanced simul- 23d Feb.
taneously from both camps, moving in
parallel columns by both banks.   Much
swift water was encountered, but no rapid
necessitating tracking.   By an early hour
in the afternoon the leading boats had
reached a cluster of grass huts at the head
of a swift rapid, said by Abu Bekr to be
named Huella, and to be the last habita-
tions in the Monassir country.

Before nightfall, by dint of great exertion,
the last boat of the column had closed up,
and our 215 boats lay moored side by side

along the bank, having averaged 10½ miles
rowing against very swift water.

The mounted troops having reconnoitred
five miles to the front, reported good clear
water, and having seen no enemy, though
traces of their camel scouts, fell back to
Huella.

The convoy and artillery, marching on a
broad front over the undulating desert sand,
also closed up.   On the way I had halted
them, and told Major Wodehouse, who
commanded the convoy throughout, to make
dispositions to resist an attack from the
left front. The camels were rapidly parked,
and a strong front of fire brought to bear ;
and I was satisfied that the convoy, which
was moving with wide-flanking scouts,
would run no risk of being taken at a dis-
advantage.   The convoy then moved on
to Huella.

Village Huella was not, in any sense of
the term, and there was no cultivation.
It was apparently only the temporary
resting-place of nomad Arabs, who brought

flocks and herds there to water and graze. There was no forage for camels, but we were assured that the following day's advance through easy water would bring us to cultivation in the Robatab country. The camels had brought loads of cut forage with them from El Kab and Hajar el Baida, and an issue of grain was sanctioned.

Shortly after leaving El Kab, we had been hailed by a camel-man on the left bank, and having ferried him across, ascertained that he was a spy sent from the Intelligence Department at headquarters, who had been sent to Berber with orders to report his news to us on his way back. It differed in little from what we previously knew. He brought back with him a messenger whom we had sent from Hebbeh on the 21st with despatches. This messenger had been seized by some dervishes in the Shukook pass, his papers had been taken from him, and he had been stripped. The dervishes were proceeding to kill him, when the camel-

Q

man from Berber appeared on the scene,
and they fled hastily.

In the evening, a boy whom we had
sent with instructions to try and reach Abu
Hamed, and bring back news, returned,
saying that he had been stopped by a party
of dervishes on the right bank about ten
miles from our camp, and made prisoner,
but had escaped. He had gathered from
them that there were only a few of the
enemy between us and Abu Hamed on this
bank, but that the Monassir and Robatab,
and a force from Berber with Suleiman
Wad Gamr and other sheikhs, were holding a rocky position on the other bank, at a
place called Shamkiyeh, near Jebel Gergerib,
and intended to oppose our advance there.
They were not aware of our having crossed
all our mounted troops to the right bank.

We bivouacked in a strong semicircular
position on the yellow sand, covering our
boats and mounted troops on the sandbank
below. At nine o'clock, being now within

the distance, we fired a rocket from the
nearest high hill, and another five minutes
later—a preconcerted signal to inform Rundle's scouts, who should be on the watch,
that we were within thirty miles of Abu
Hamed. I walked round the position, and
saw that perfect order reigning which came
from the constant repetition and constant
supervision of the nightly bivouac in readiness to meet instantaneous attack. Troops
peacefully sleeping, tired with the hard
day's work, beside their piled arms; double
sentries alert and motionless, watching with
trained eyes every foot of the open space
before the bivouac; officers on watch vig-
ilant; perfect silence everywhere. Not once,
in any camp I had been in, had there ever
been a sign of a false alarm. This day's
work had been the best ever performed by
the troops. Two hundred and fifteen boats
had been rowed by their strong arms
through ten or eleven miles of the swiftest water possible to contend with. Our

wounded were all doing well. No death
had occurred among them since we left our
camp at Dulka. The physical condition of
the men was magnificent. We had completed a month out from Hamdab—a month
of almost unparalleled exertion, passed entirely in the open air. We had not sent
back one sick man; we had had but one
death from disease; and the total sick-list of
the force was now only eighteen, a proportion of 6.4 per 1000—a condition of health
which I believe to be unprecedented among
any troops in any campaign. The men
were in high spirits; and there were two
battalions, neither of which had yet been in
action, longing for the chance of emulating
those who had fought so gallantly at Kirbekan. It was the first time I had seen
the whole force in one bivouac; and I lay
down with a feeling of perfect confidence in
their power to conquer any host of Arabs
that the Mahdi could bring against them
from the farthest corners of the Soudan.

In four days, I said to myself, we shall be
at Abu Hamed. We shall open up the
Korosko desert-route, and our doing so
will ring through the Soudan, and weak-
en the knees of the followers of Mahomet
Achmet.

CHAPTER XV.

RECALL—BACK TO SALAMAT.

24th Feb. I HAD issued orders that to give the men more rest after so good a day's work, *réveillé* would not sound till half-past five; and it was seven o'clock on the morning of the 24th before the first boat was in readiness to move. Some letters and Reuter's telegrams had arrived the night before by camel-post; and an opportunity thus occurring of sending back to Korti, I reported in the most cheerful terms to Lord Wolseley. Seeking for something in my despatch-box, I came across the following cutting which I had taken at Halfa from the 'Army and Navy Gazette' of the 13th September 1884 :—

"The opinions which were expressed in this

journal as soon as the orders were made known
for the construction of those ridiculous row-boats
for the expedition on the Nile have been cor-
roborated by the assent and concurrence of every
man who has any experience of the country and
the river. A more wicked waste of money was
never perpetrated, a more silly quackery was
never devised, by any public department than that
of which Lord Hartington and the Duke of Cam-
bridge, representing the War Office and the Horse
Guards, have really and truly been guilty in
ordering that monstrous armada of boats, that
unfloatable flotilla for the Nile! Burn them for
firewood! Send them to Jericho, to ply on the
Palestine canal of the future! Make matches of
them — do anything with them! Put men in
them, and try to send them up the Nile cataracts
—never, we beg of you!"

Well, there they lay, 215 boats of the
unfloatable flotilla, floating above all the
worst cataracts of the Nile, within ten
miles of the last of that series of rapids of
which it was said in every map published
before the expedition started, "Between
Gerendid and Mograt cataracts (140 miles),
the river is unnagivable at low Nile." Said,

and truly said hitherto. It had been left for British soldiers and British "ridiculous row - boats" to navigate the unnavigable, and to convey an army of 3000 men, with their stores and munitions of war, to within twenty-six miles of Abu Hamed.

Our cavalry scouts and patrols had long been out. The leading boats of the Gordons had just pushed off. The main body of the cavalry had moved out of camp. Colonel Butler was riding past my bivouac, when a messenger arrived with a despatch from Korti. I opened it. It was mostly in cipher; but some words in clear caught my eye, sent a cold shiver through me, and caused me at once to sound the halt.

This is what the message said when it had been deciphered :—

"KORTI, 20th February.

"Buller evacuated Gubat. His main body went to Gakdul with all sick and wounded. He remains with about 1500 men at Abu Klea. The enemy have now begun to fire into his camp there, and have killed and wounded some of his men. He awaits camels to fall back on Gakdul,

which I hope he will begin to do to-morrow, the
21st instant; but owing to the weak state of his
camels, all his men must go on foot. I have
abandoned all hope of going to Berber before
the autumn campaign begins. You will therefore not go to Abu Hamed, but having burned
and destroyed everything in the neighbourhood
where Stewart was murdered, you will withdraw
all your force to Abu Dom, near Merawi, bringing all the Mudir's troops with you.

" Please express to the troops Lord Wolseley's
high appreciation of their gallant conduct in
action, and of the military spirit they have dis-
played in overcoming the great difficulties presented by the river. Having punished the
Monassir people for Stewart's murder, it is not
intended to-undertake any further military operations until after the approaching hot season.

" Further orders will be sent to you upon your
reaching Abu Dom. Until you have occupied
the Shukook pass, and made sure of every one
through it, you had better keep this telegram
entirely to yourself and Butler. Of course, if you
are in the presence of the enemy when you
receive this, you must defeat him before turning
back. If you do not receive this before you
have reached Abu Hamed, or are so near to it
that it is merely a question of occupying it without opposition, you must halt there, and send

back information at once to me, when I will start
the convoy from Korosko, which I do not otherwise mean to despatch. Of course it is impossible
at this distance to give you positive orders, but
Lord Wolseley has every confidence in your
military discretion."

But little time was needed for decision.
The cup was snatched from our lips, but
we must bear the disappointment bravely.
The conditions in which I found myself
gave no reasonable excuse for pressing on.
And lightly as the message touched upon
General Buller's difficulties, there was sufficient in it to give cause for anxiety as to
the result of his retreat.   That he had not
retired one hour before it was necessary to
do so was a certainty.   If his troops should
be surrounded by vast numbers of the late
besiegers of Khartoum, who had already
had three weeks within which to collect to
oppose him, his situation might be full of
peril.   I knew Lord Wolseley could have
but a handful of men at Korti, and the
flower of his force was here in the River

Column. I had but one course open to me
—to make my way to Abu Dom with all
possible speed. I showed the telegram to
Colonel Butler. He entirely agreed with
me, and I sent back the following reply :—

" I received your telegram this morning, just as
the troops were starting up river. I am, by the
map, about twenty-six miles from Abu Hamed.
I am not in the immediate presence of the enemy,
nor have the patrols, who have been six miles
beyond this, had any touch of the enemy. Nor
do I anticipate meeting the enemy to-day, should
I continue my advance. My latest information
is that the enemy intend to fight at Abu Hamed,
and I anticipate opposition if I advance upon it.
There is a cataract between me and Abu Hamed,
and if opposed, it might take some days before I
could occupy the place. I am confident I could
beat any force opposed to me, but I feel it my
duty, in view of the facts contained in the first
part of your telegram, to fall back immediately
to Abu Dom, and I shall fall back to Hebbeh
to-day. I shall return by the right bank."

By returning along the right bank to
Merawi, I should avoid all danger of opposition to the convoy in the Shukook pass,

where a few men could cause serious delay.
It was evidently impossible for any serious
opposition to be organised at very short
notice on the right bank.

I then issued the following orders to the
troops : "The Brigadier-General announces
to the troops that since they entered the
boats this morning he has received a telegram from Lord Wolseley, stating that,
after the Monassir tribe has been punished
for Colonel Stewart's murder, it is not intended to undertake any further military
operations until after the approaching hot
season. The furthest limits of the Monassir
country having been reached, and the punishment for Colonel Stewart's murder having been, so far as possible, inflicted, the
troops will now return through the Monassir
country to Birti. The column will therefore move upon Hebbeh to-day." Lord
Wolseley's expression of appreciation was
also published, and the following was added : "The Brigadier-General has to remind
the troops that the descent of this swift

river will require even greater care than its ascent. All will depend upon the vigilance of the men in the bows, and the coolness and resource of the men steering."

The following instructions for the information of officers in charge of boats descending the Nile were drawn up by Lieut.-Colonel Alleyne :—

" 1. Owing to the swiftness of the stream, the boats will move over it at a rapid rate, consequently if a boat strikes a rock she will probably receive a severe injury. Accidents of this nature can be avoided, *first*, by the vigilance of the poleman, who should sound frequently ; *secondly*, by not allowing boats to close up or crowd upon each other when descending a rapid.

" 2. As a rule, when descending a rapid the crew must row, otherwise the boat will not steer.

" 3. The last two (2) boats of each battalion should be nearly empty, so that in the event of a boat being severely injured in a rapid, they may be able to take in her cargo or return to her assistance. All other boats should have equal draught of water.

" 4. Coxwains must follow the lead given by boats with pilots in them.

" 5. After descending a rapid, the leading boats must halt until the rear boats join them.

" In difficult rapids special arrangements will be made for taking each boat through with Canadian pilots."

While halted, I was informed that a number of men on camels had been seen in the desert to the south-west. Patrols were sent out, but the camels turned out to be only the product of a fevered imagination. However, some delay had been caused; and so the men were ordered to dine early, and then move down-stream. The mounted troops were ordered to patrol up-stream and cover the retirement by a forward reconnaissance, while the convoy with an escort returned towards Hebbeh. At noon the boats commenced to move downstream, led by Colonel Denison commanding the Canadian voyageurs. The column moved in reversed order from its progress up-stream. The Staffords led, followed successively by the Black Watch and Cornwalls. The Gordons brought up the rear.

The three leading battalions reached
Hebbeh, and bivouacked on the high Nile
island.   The Gordons were halted with the
convoy, camel battery, and part of the
camel corps at Umsyal, a village three
miles above Hebbeh, where there was plenty of good forage, with orders to destroy
houses and *sakyehs* before leaving.   The
cavalry and the remainder of the camel
corps having patrolled to within sight of
the island of Mograt and seen no enemy,
halted at El Kab, under Colonel Butler.

The casualties amongst the boats were
three damaged and repaired, and one total
wreck.   The horses and camels had suffered
heavily from the heat, and the heavy sand
fetlock-deep.   Four camels and one horse
died of exhaustion.   I therefore ordered a
halt for the next day, except that all the
troops and convoy were to close up to
Hebbeh.

The evening brought a messenger with
despatches, all of earlier date than that received in the morning, and not containing

orders of recall; also messages from the Commandant at Abu Dom and the Vakeel, to say that neither for love nor money could they get any more messengers to come to us. It did not matter now; we were going to them. But I have often since thought, that if that messenger had not been so pressing who reached us with the order of recall, we should have been in presence of the enemy; we should have had another fight, and as we had twice as many troops present as at Kirbekan, probably an even more telling victory. I must then have occupied Abu Hamed; and the fact of our doing so would, I believe, have materially improved our position in the Soudan. But fate willed it otherwise.

25th Feb.   On the 25th the troops were employed in completing the destruction of the houses and *sakyehs* of the village of Hebbeh, and on the island of El Kun, and the Gordons and mounted troops closed up on the column.

A detachment of Hussars and camel

corps was sent to a village about three
miles down-stream, with orders to march
off at the same hour as the boats in the
morning. Supplies were equalised among
the regiments, in proportion to their number
of boats, and ordered to be so divided as to
bring all boats to as nearly as possible the
same draught of water.

Orders were issued to the following effect :
The Gordons were to move off at 7.45 A.M.,
followed at successive intervals of three-
quarters of an hour by the Staffords, Black
Watch, and Cornwalls—the last regiment
furnishing the rear-guard. In every battalion except the rear battalion, the officer
second in command was to bring up the .
rear of his battalion, being held responsible
for bringing on all boats of his own battalion, and all boats of details moving with
his battalion or between it and the preceding battalion. He was not to move on
himself until every one of these boats that
could be brought on had preceded him.
Each battalion, as previously ordered, was

R

to have two empty boats moving in rear of the others.

The officer commanding the rear battalion was himself to bring up the rear of the whole column. He was to tell off four companies of his battalion as a rear-guard, and to move with this rear-guard in rear of all boats not abandoned, being held responsible that no boat of the column was left behind unless necessarily abandoned, and that all abandoned boats were destroyed. On arrival in camp he was to report verbally to headquarters that every boat had arrived.

Major Flood, 12th Hussars, was to cover the rear of the column with the mounted troops; and the command of the rear-guard on shore and on the river was given to Colonel Butler, to whom the officer commanding the rear battalion was to report, should he be unable to reach headquarters camp.

The number of repairing boats was increased to four,—one to move in rear of

each battalion, and assist in repairing any
boats that might be damaged, and could
not be repaired regimentally.

In reporting to Lord Wolseley in the
evening, I said that, after consultation with
Butler and Alleyne, I was of opinion it
would take six or seven days to Birti, and
six or seven from that place to Merawi.
My place of crossing would depend on the
information I might receive at Birti.

On the morning of the 26th the troops 26th Feb.
moved as ordered. By noon the advanced
guard of mounted troops and the convoy,
with two battalions of infantry, were concentrated at Amarim, opposite Salamat, on
the right bank, near the head of Sherri
island. We on the bank rode along a flat
wady at some distance from the bank the
greater part of the way. On reaching
Amarim, I at once rode on with Alleyne
and Peel to inspect the channel between
the right bank and Sherri island. We found
it impracticable for boats from its shallowness, and the distance of the right bank

from the left bank of the river increased
rapidly, it being evident that very large
islands lay between.

I was satisfied that it would be now
practically impossible to combine with accuracy the movements of the mounted
troops and of the boats. We were now
about to commence the descent of the formidable series of cataracts between Salamat
and Ooli; and I decided that my own
proper place was with the boats, and that
the command of the mounted troops and
convoy should be confided to Colonel Butler. Moving a cavalry advanced guard
about three miles down-stream, and leaving
the remainder at Amarim, where I halted
the Cornwalls on their arrival for the purpose of completing the mounted troops up
to six days' rations from the boats, I instructed Colonel Butler to advance at 7 A.M.
on the 27th, sending the Cornwalls by river
at the same hour. He was to endeavour
to keep touch of the troops in boats, but
failing that, to make his way to Hush el

Jeruf, opposite Birti, and await the boats
there.   Each party was to fire a rocket at
8 P.M. each night to show the other its
position.

My brigade-major and aide - de - camp
were to accompany me in the boats; all
other staff officers, except the boat officers,
to accompany the party on shore.   Colvile
was instructed, as soon as he thought it
safe, to join the Vakeel at Birti, inform him
I had received Lord Wolseley's orders to
move to Abu Dom and take his troops with
me, and request him to be ready to march
immediately on my arrival.

These orders issued, I entered one of the
boats of the headquarter escort Gordon
Highlanders, and by sunset the three battalions were in bivouac on Sherri island.
One boat of the Staffords struck a rock,
and had to be abandoned as a total wreck.
Arms, ammunition, and most of her stores
were saved; no lives were lost.

A native who had ·hailed us from the left
bank opposite Hebbeh in the morning, was

brought on in the boats, and on being questioned in the evening, told the following story. He was one of the soldiers of the Mudir, and had been taken prisoner at Ambukol by the Shagiyeh, and sold to Haddai in the previous summer. When Haddai was killed, he was taken to Mograt—not to the island, but to the mainland on the left bank— where he worked for a man named Mohammed el Amin, a dervish. In the evening of the 25th, hearing the English were near, he escaped, and travelled by the left bank till he got opposite our boats in the morning. He said that at Shamkiyeh there were assembled Suleiman Wad Gamr with the Monassir, and Wad Abu Hegel with the Robatab, and many men from Berber under Lekalik, all under the chief command of Abu Hegel; that at this place the river passes through a narrow passage between rocks, and there is an old fort on each bank; that they had fortified the rocks with stone-work, and occupied these old forts, and intended to dispute the advance of our boats. They had no artillery, and but few rifles, but they were numerous,—far more numerous than our force, — and had all either swords or spears. They had heard of Kirbekan, and knew that Moussa Wad Abu Hegel and many dervishes had been killed. They knew also that Khartoum had fallen, and Gordon had been killed. They told the people that Gordon was killed because he refused to become a Mussulman, and that the English, when they saw so many dervishes, would all throw their arms into the river from fear. They had heard, he said, of our returning; and when he left their camp the previous night, they were loading up provisions on camels, with the intention of following us.

On our way down, we saw signs of a hasty retreat having been made from Sherri island. There were a few native boats, all of which we destroyed, as we had done all we could find coming up the river; and there were some rough rafts. The whaler abandoned by Captain Peel on the 16th was found hauled up, and the stores that had been left with her were gone. Several natives were seen watching us from behind distant rocks, but we were in no way molested.

CHAPTER XVI.

RUNNING THE RAPIDS—BACK TO HAMDAB.

THE boat officers had decided that it would 26th Feb. be impossible to pass down the left-bank channel by which we had ascended the Sherari rapid; and accordingly we had turned out of the left-bank channel, and our bivouac on Sherri island was on a central channel between Sherri and Sherari, at the head of a rapid. In the descent of the river a different nature of channel had to be sought from that best suited for ascent. In ascending, wherever the river became too swift for rowing, passages had to be sought through which the boats could be hauled or tracked, and these necessarily were never in mid-stream, but always close to the bank,

either of the main shore or of an island.   A
very great rush of water was to be avoided ;
and in consequence of these requirements,
the passage by which the boats ascended a
rapid was generally very shallow, and frequently only a narrow channel among rocks.
To attempt to descend by such passages as
these would be to court certain destruction
for the boats; and the main point was to
find sufficient depth of water, no matter how
swift or turbulent the stream.   Consequently,
as a rule, the descent was in mid-stream of
that channel which, in their upward journey,
the boat officer had noted as most likely to
be full of water.

I had originally intended to make the
battalions in turn take the onerous duty of
furnishing the rear-guard; but on considering the question, I decided to make the
advanced guard and rear-guard permanent,
chiefly because any other arrangement in-
volving the transposition of battalions in
the order of the column might involve delay.
Having selected Colonel Hammill to com-

mand the advanced guard of Gordon Highlanders and the naval boat, and Colonel
Green the rear - guard of Black Watch,
orders were issued for the descent of the
rapids in the following order — Gordons,
Cornwalls, Staffords, Black Watch, commencing at 6.45 A.M.

Instructions were issued by Alleyne for
the passing of the Sherri island rapid to
the following effect :—

" The two boats of each battalion that are
first passed down the rapid will not put into
shore, but remain in the stream at the foot
of the rapid, one near each bank, ready to
pull to any boat that may require assistance,—an officer and life-belts to be in each
boat. The two boats of the leading battalion to be relieved by the two leading
boats of the following battalion, and so on.

" The first set of boats will be taken
through the rapid by Canadian voyageurs ;
and a company officer will descend in each
boat, who, on his return, should be able to
steer a boat of his company down the rapid.

After the first set of boats have passed the rapid, a Canadian will be placed in every second, third, or fourth boat, as may be found necessary. At the hour named to start, adjutants of battalions will collect the voyageurs of battalions, and hand them over to Lieutenant-Colonel Denison.

" When the boats have passed the rapid they will be anchored on the sandbank on the right bank till that anchorage is full, when they will be anchored on the sandbank on the left bank.

" The life-buoys in all boats to be always so placed that they can be thrown without delay to a man in the water."

27th Feb. The rapid was run by all the boats of the column by 10.30 A.M., with the exception of the rear-guard and the rear boats of the Cornwalls, who were delayed by a boat of the Cornwalls which, in descending from Amarim, was wrecked above our Sherri island bivouac on a sunken rock. Her crew, arms (except one rifle), ammunition, and stores were saved. The boat

was got to shore, but so badly damaged
that she had to be broken up and burnt;
and it was 1.30 P.M. before the whole of
the boats were through and concentrated
about a mile and a half above the bivouac
of Shoar on the upward journey. The
column then moved forward, well closed
up, to the head of Uss rapid. Here it
was decided not to attempt the left-bank
channel, but to pass round the western side
of Little Uss island. A sharp short rapid,
with a nasty curve, had to be run at the
turning from the left-bank channel, into the
passage between the two islands; and the
naval boat, which was one of the first to
attempt the passage, struck heavily on a
rock in mid-stream, in the swiftest water,
and remained there. Other boats were
with difficulty taken to her assistance by
the voyageurs, her stores were unloaded,
and she was got off; but in getting her off,
a boat of the Gordon Highlanders got on
the rock, and in freeing her, another boat
of the Gordons was so damaged that she

filled and sank. This accident to the naval boat caused considerable delay, as, while the other boats were engaged in rescuing her, and the boats damaged in going to her help, the passage of the rapid was blocked. Thus by nightfall only 64 boats, Gordons and part of Cornwalls, were through the rapid; and the force bivouacked in two camps above and below the rapid on Uss island, about 1000 yards apart. A few natives with spears were seen, but they all kept out of our way. We fired our signal rocket at 8 P.M., and were answered by Colonel Butler from the mainland, about two miles due west.

Our total wrecks this day were three,— one of the Gordons and one of the Cornwalls, already described, and another of the Cornwalls, which struck on the rocks and filled almost immediately after leaving the Sherri island bivouac. The repairing parties worked till late in the night, repairing other boats more or less seriously damaged.

The following day would take us into

the Shukook, where, if anywhere, the
enemy would attempt to interfere with our
passage. There were many places where
the river passed between rocky cliffs, from
which a few riflemen could do us serious
damage. I did not for a moment anticipate that any large force would be gathered
there; but I did think it highly probable
that the enemy would post a small body
of riflemen to oppose our passage, and that
we might have to land a force to turn them
out. Orders were therefore issued that two
men would be in the bows of each boat
with their rifles loaded and in their hands,
and with accoutrements and ammunition
ready. In the event of any shots being
fired at the boats, these men were at once
to return the fire. The column was not
to be halted for mere stray shots; but
should any serious amount of firing take
place, the nearest boats were at once to
pull to shore and land their men, the
landing being covered by the armed bowmen. Wooden plugs were made and issued

out to each boat to stop bullet-holes if required.

Previous to the advance on the morning of 28th, I saw commanding officers, and explained to them my wishes in case of our being fired upon, and of a landing being necessary. We then moved off, halting at the foot of the Uss rapid till two battalions and a half were concentrated there, and then recommencing the advance. My endeavour was throughout this descent of the river, as in the ascent, so to regulate the movement as to obtain the greatest possible rapidity consistent with power of concentration to meet any sudden attack. The advance through the Shukook was unmolested. As my boat followed the last company of the Gordons, I was in momentary expectation of hearing the first shots fired. It would have been so easy to shoot some of our men in the boats from the rocky cliffs, and to choose places for the riflemen whence they could easily escape before we could reach them with

our infantry. But not a shot was fired,
and not a human being was seen; and it
was with no small satisfaction that we
emerged from the rocky defile, and, having
passed our old camp at Wady el Argu, ran
the very nasty rapid intervening between
it and the high Nile island camp at Kirbekan, which we reached at 11.30 A.M.
This rapid required that every boat should
be taken down by voyageurs, and occa-
sioned considerable delay. At night the
Gordon Highlanders and my headquarters reached Dulka island, and bivouacked
there, immediately opposite the old camp
whence we had marched for our fight, and
the remaining troops bivouacked between
the old Kirbekan camp and Wady el Argu.
Our rocket was answered by Colonel Butler
about six miles W.N.W. He was encamped
on the north bank, opposite Birti island.
We had got through the day without the
loss of a boat.

While halted in the afternoon at the high
Nile island camp of Kirbekan, the Gordons

s

had taken prisoner an old man, dressed in the Mahdi's patchwork uniform. He gave no information, and next·day I handed him over to the Vakeel, who pronounced him old and half-witted, and let him go. A messenger from Birti brought me word that the Vakeel had gone to El Koua with some of the troops, but was expected back in the morning. Achmet Effendi, the commander of the troops, was deeply concerned at our return, and begged me to let him know its cause.

1st March. On the 1st March, as soon as the troops had closed up to Dulka island, we continued our advance. We successfully passed the troublesome rapid above Castle Camp, and the swift water above Birti. I took Colonel Butler on board off Birti island, and dropped down to his camp, where I was joined by Colonel Colvile, who had seen the Vakeel, and arranged for his starting as soon as ordered to do so. The boats of the column pressed on to their rendezvous on the right bank, opposite the

site of our old bivouac, where the Vakeel
was now in camp.

The Vakeel, accompanied by Achmet
Effendi, now crossed over to see me; and
it was arranged with him that he should
start on the following morning.   There was
a short desert-route from Birti to Jebel
Kulgeili, but he preferred marching near
the river, and keeping touch of our boats.
Colvile now again joined the Vakeel's
camp, with instructions to await our arrival
at Hamdab.   I sent off a messenger reporting arrival to Lord Wolseley.

Having rationed the mounted troops up
to six days, the boats again moved on, and
entered the Rahami cataract, where we
were again obliged to place a voyageur in
every boat.   Each time that the nature of
the rapids required this caused delay—as
after taking a boat down, each voyageur
had to walk back to the head of the rapid
to bring down another boat.   We had only
sixty-seven voyageurs, and more than two
hundred boats; so when only one voyageur

was required for a boat, each had to make from three to four trips; when two were required, each had to make seven trips.

Headquarters, Cornwalls, and Staffords bivouacked on the left bank, about the middle of the cataract; the Gordons on a sandy island opposite; and the Black Watch, who had not yet entered the cataract, about three-quarters of a mile above.

The men were now becoming as skilful in the descent as they had become in the ascent of the rapids. An excellent system of leaving boats at important places to point out the route to be taken had been perfected by Colonel Alleyne. Boats followed at regular intervals keeping to the track of the pilot-boat, and the words "slower" or "faster" were passed down the line with rapidity. But we could not avoid accidents : two boats of the Staffords had to be abandoned to-day, and two were badly damaged, but repaired. Still, we had lost no lives, and but few stores.

2d March.   On the 2d the advance was resumed.

Rahami cataract was successfully negotiated;
and we entered the swift water at the top
of Umhaboah cataract. Near our old camp
at Warag we were halted, while Colonels
Denison and Alleyne examined the river
in front. Alleyne returned presently and
told me there was a choice between two
passages. That to the right was straight,
but there was a clear fall of nearly three feet
at one place. That to the left had no
actual waterfall, but it was a rushing inclined plane, its worst feature being that
the channel was narrow, and turned at
right angles in the very worst part of the
shoot. They had elected for this latter
passage; but considered no one should
descend it except the necessary two voyageurs (bowman and steerer), and the six
men required to row each boat. All others
were ordered to walk, and all arms were
portaged.

The voyageurs walked to see the shoot,
before attempting to pass it. They said it
was bad, but practicable. To me it seemed

as bad as bad could be. The channel
to the left, and then sharply at right
to the right.   Just at this turn, two
rocks stood out in mid-stream.   ]
necessary to pass between them.   Th
error in steering would be fatal.   To
the turn too soon would bring the b⸱
to the right-hand rock; to wait to⸱
would sweep her on to the left-han⸱
Sitting under the shadow of a great ⸱
watched this triumph of skill over a di⸱
that to any one unaccustomed to sucl
would have seemed insuperable.   Bo⸱
boat came down at lightning-spee
men giving way with might and n
give steering power; the bowmen st
cool and collected watching the wat⸱
only using the oar should the ste⸱
seem to need help; the steersmen b⸱
round the boat with marvellous ju⸱
at the right moment.   Now and tl
error of half a second brought a boa
the edge of the left-hand rock, and sl
and fell like a horse jumping a fence

in the day's work only one boat of the
Gordons and one of the Staffords were
wrecked. Half the force bivouacked below
this shoot at our old camp of Mishami
ridge; half above it at Warag.

The Mudir's troops bivouacked at Kab
el Abd, and we established heliographic
communication with Colonel Butler at
Shebabit. We had entered again into the
land of the friendly Shagiyehs, and the first
sakyeh we had seen at work since leaving
Hamdab groaned out its creaking welcome
to us opposite Gamra.

The two rear battalions were ordered
to close up on the following morning, the
advance of the leading battalions to be
postponed till this was complete.

Early in the morning the passage of this 3d March.
rapid was continued. As one boat was
coming through, her rudder broke; she
struck a rock, and the voyageur in the bow
was thrown by the shock into the water.
He, fortunately, clung to the rock, and got
upon it. A boat was lowered down to him

by a rope from the shore by other voyageurs, and he was brought safely to land. This, and the length of time required for the return-trips of the voyageurs, made it half-past eleven before all boats were through, and in readiness to advance.

Passing through Kab el Abd, we looked in vain for the cataract that was "like the big gate of Semneh" as we went up. It had entirely disappeared. This was only one of the many striking changes in the nature and appearance of the river between our ascent and descent. The Nile evidently entirely changes its character at each place with its change of level, and no map of the river drawn at any one season can be even approximately correct for another season. We made good progress to the head of the fourth cataract. Here again it was decided not to attempt the channel to the west of Suffi island by which the boats had ascended, but to descend the main channel on the left bank. It was a long straight run of a mile and a half or more (distances are hard to measure when flying like an express train) of water broken and rough, studded with rocks both seen and unseen— a dangerous rapid to the unskilled or care-less, yet safe to the trained eye and skilled hand.

As my boat shot down we passed the adjutant of the Gordons, with his boat stuck fast in the very centre of the boiling rapid—a useful beacon to the following boats. His was not the only boat that struck. Four others of the same battalion were on rocks. Three were repaired, but two of the five sank and were abandoned. The quartermaster was thrown into the water, and lost all his kit. The adjutant had a narrow escape for his life. Thrown into the water, as his boat sank, his head struck a sharp rock, and he was severely cut. The arms, ammunition, and men's bedding in his boat, and all lives, were saved. The Black Watch, also, had to abandon a boat that struck on a rock near Kabour. But by sunset, thanks to the admirable exertions of the men, and the skill of the voyageurs, all wrecked crews were brought to shore. All the Gordons and eleven boats of the Cornwalls bivouacked below the rapid, and the remainder of the troops above.

The Mudir's troops encamped half a mile north of us on the left bank; Colonel Butler's party on the right bank, opposite the end of Ooli island.

Orders were issued for the troops to close up below the cataract before advancing in the morning; and to Colonel Butler to march to Abu Dom, select a place and make preparations for his crosssing.

4th March. On the 4th the remaining boats passed through the fourth cataract with a loss of three boats wrecked, and, alas! with the first fatal accident in all our downward journey. The course to be steered through the cataract was a very tortuous one. The boats had to go from mid-stream over close to the right bank, and there pass between a rock and the shore, turning again to the left into mid-stream. Officers and a voyageur were stationed with their boats on the rocky islands to show the direction to be taken, but unfortunately a boat stuck across the stream, in the narrow channel near the right bank, blocking it. Instead of the remaining boats being turned in to the bank to wait till the channel was clear, they were by some error directed off into mid-stream, and the greater part of the boats of three battalions shot over a fall of about three feet, like a Thames weir in flood. That only one accident occurred is marvellous. One boat having safely shot the weir, through some error in steering struck a rock violently, and upset. Unfortunately she had in her two wounded men, both of whom, with a sergeant, were drowned. One of the wounded men, private Barber, had been specially distinguished by his gallant conduct at Kirbekan. A wounded private of the Black Watch also died on board his boat in passing through the cataract. His leg had been amputated above the knee, and it was an almost hopeless case.

It was nearly noon before the running of this rapid was complete, and we then moved down the river. A halt was made at Jebel Kulgeili, to concentrate two battalions, and the advance was continued to Hamdab, where three and a half battalions concentrated in bivouac. The rear-guard half-battalion Black Watch, with two damaged boats of the Staffords and six of the Cornwalls, were still in rear.

The Mudir's troops bivouacked at Dugiyet; the mounted troops at Kasingar, opposite Belal.

We had descended in nine days what it had taken us thirty-one days to ascend.

CHAPTER XVII.

THE BREAK-UP OF THE COLUMN—BACK TO KORTI.

AT Hamdab I received a telegram from Korti. General Buller's name at the head was sufficient to tell us the retreat had been safely accomplished from Abu Klea. The telegram directed me to leave Colonel Butler in command at Abu Dom with the Black Watch, a troop of Hussars, the Egyptian camel corps, two guns of the Egyptian battery, a detachment of Engineers, and a hundred transport camels, with all the rations I could spare, and to bring the rest of the column to Korti.

On the morning of the 5th we moved 5th March. on to Abu Dom. The rapid water between

Hamdab and Belal offered no difficulty of importance, and by 12.30 P.M. two battalions had closed up, and the mounted troops had reached the right bank at Merawi. At 1.40 P.M., after the men's dinners, the boats of the Gordons and Staffords commenced to take across the animals and their loads, and by sunset the greater number of them were across, and all the infantry in bivouac together.

The Mudir's troops I had halted at Duaim, three miles short of Abu Dom. Orders arrived for them to be sent to hold Hamdab, for which place, on my recommendation, Dugiyet was afterwards substituted, as being nearer the supplies of Belal, and at the entrance of the Berber road.

6th March. The early part of the 6th was occupied in ferrying across the remainder of the animals, and in the transfer of supplies from the regiments going to Korti to the commissariat officer detailed to remain at Abu Dom. A committee consisting of Colonel Butler, Colonel Alleyne, Lieutenant-Colonel

Colvile, Major Slade, Captain Courtenay,
and Lieutenant Colborne, met and went
over the survey together, deciding upon the
names of the various cataracts, islands, villages, hills, and districts through which we
had passed. This was no easy task, as the
same places seem to be known by many different names; and when the sound of a
name was agreed upon, it was no easy matter to spell the word. Major Colborne's
map, attached to this volume, represents the
fruit of their joint revision.

A violent dust-storm blew throughout the
day, but dropped towards evening ; and at
five o'clock I held a review of the River
Column—the first and the last time it was
ever inspected on parade. The horses,
though their feet were tender from want of
shoes, did not show any other signs of un-
fitness. The camels of the camel corps
and battery seemed none the worse for
their crossing. Two thousand of the finest
fighting men that it ever was any man's lot
to command were inspected in line, marched

past, re-formed in line of quarter-columns, and advanced in review order. Having said a few farewell words to commanding officers, I bade the column, as " The River Column," good-bye.

The voyageurs were drawn up at the flag-staff under command of Lieutenant-Colonel Denison. Out of the contingent of 377 men that left Canada, ten had died, six of whom had been drowned in the Nile. Their six months' engagement expiring on 9th March, eighty-nine of them had re-engaged, and sixty-seven of those had ascended the Nile with the River Column. ·Without them, the ascent of the river, if not impossible, would have been far slower, and attended with far greater loss of life. Without them, the descent of the river would have been impossible. Officers and men, they had worked with unceasing energy and a complete disregard of danger.

The Vakeel had been met at Duaim by an order for him at once to hand over his duties to Izzedin Bey, and to consider himself dismissed. Another commander was also being sent up to replace Achmet Effendi. Both these acts appear to have been the Mudir's own, without reference to Lord Wolseley. The first, the dismissal of the Vakeel, was beyond his powers; and the Vakeel was reinstated later, and sent to replace the Mudir himself at Dongola. As soon as he saw that the English were really strong and in earnest, he had done his best to help us. I had no fault to find with him, or with Achmet Effendi, and I publicly thanked them on the parade, at which they both were present.

Achmet Effendi, however, expressed strong objections to being sent to garrison Dugiyet. The fact was, that information had arrived that the enemy reoccupied Birti the day after the Mudir's troops left it. Rumour exaggerated their numbers; and a force of 6000 men was said to be there under Lekalik, Suleiman Wad Gamr,

T

and Abu Hegel, while an army under Mohammed El Kheir was said to be advancing from Berber by the river to join them.

On the morning of the 7th, having said good-bye to Butler and his troops, I started with the boats, and early on the 8th handed over my command at Korti. The River Column then ceased to exist.

In justice to those on whom the great burden of the work fell, I will end this narrative with the last paragraph of my final report to Lord Wolseley: "I cannot," I said, "close this report without dwelling upon the splendid behaviour of the regimental officers, non-commissioned officers, and men of this column. The life of the men has been one of incessant toil from the first to the last day of the expedition. In ragged clothing, scarred and blistered by the sun and rough work, they have worked with constant cheerfulness and unceasing

energy. Their discipline has been beyond
reproach ; and I do not hesitate to say that
no finer, more gallant, or more trustworthy
body of men ever served the Queen than
those I have had the honour to command
in the River Column."

THE END.

PRINTED BY WILLIAM BLACKWOOD AND SONS.